PRAISE

Joey Asher's coaching and ideas have helped the sales force at The Weather Channel and *Weather.com* learn how to win business. Using the five fundamentals detailed in this book, we have been able to deliver great sales presentations and win more business. Use the ideas in this book and you'll get great results.

—Paul Iaffaldano, EVP and General Manager,
The Weather Channel Media Solutions

If you like winning, you will want to read this book. Joey Asher's simple, no nonsense advice has made a difference in my own presentations. This book is bound to improve the presentations of anyone who reads it.

—Charles F. Bowman, Finance Business Executive and the
North Carolina Market President, Bank of America

Joey Asher's hands-on approach to coaching and his ideas have helped ChoicePoint deliver superior sales presentations that gain executive attention and ultimately win business. The ideas in this book are simple fundamentals and easy to apply. Most important, they work.

—Jim Zimbardi, SVP, ChoicePoint, Inc.

Joey Asher and the ideas he presents in this book have been instrumental in helping our company win projects.

—Rob Burton, President of Hoar Construction

This is a great book. The concepts, ideas, and examples in *How to Win a Pitch* confirmed the things we are doing well and reminded me of the things we need to be doing better. To win you must improve yourself—your customers deserve it. This book helps you discover ways to solve problems for your clients and win more for you.

—Paul Silver, managing director, Huron Consulting Group
National consulting firm with offices nationwide
and around the world

Joey Asher and the ideas he presents in this book have been instrumental in helping our company win projects. It is an invaluable guide for the preparation and delivery of a successful presentation. Following his five fundamentals has resulted in our firm winning several major design commissions. Use these ideas and you'll be in the best position to distinguish yourself from the competition and win your next pitch.

—Steven Clem, Principal, tvsdesign.

At Robins & Morton we have been using Joey and his ideas for many years. The ideas in *How to Win a Pitch* have made a big difference in how we develop and present proposals. His methodology has been a major contributor to the high win-rate we have experienced over the years. I heartily recommend you read his book and apply the techniques he describes.

—Bill Morton, President and CEO of Robins & Morton

How To
WIN
A Pitch

How To
WIN
A Pitch

The Five Fundamentals
That Will Distinguish You
from the Competition

JOEY ASHER

Persuasive Speaker Press

To the men in my family who taught me how to sell.

My grandfather Joe Asher sold men's clothes in Atlanta and was instrumental in growing the menswear department at Rich's department store. He was the snappiest dresser in town. He taught me that first impressions count and that you can't catch a fish unless your line is in the water.

My grandfather Bill Savitt built Savitt Jewelers into a Hartford institution and wore wristwatches on his ankles. His store motto was "Peace of Mind, Guaranteed." He always said "Pitch, don't bitch, and don't switch."

My father Tom Asher started as a stockbroker making cold calls with Goodbody & Co. in Atlanta and recently retired as a senior executive with Smith Barney. He taught a generation of financial advisors how to sell and is revered by thousands of successful brokers as "the Dean." My dad taught me that persistence and determination count for a lot in this world.

CONTENTS

ACKNOWLEDGEMENTS

I couldn't have written this book without the wonderful Speechworks team. I'd like to thank our coaches Marilyn Ringo, Carmen Burns, Nancy Thomas, Nancy Vason, Meg Altenderfer, and Lizzie Crawford. They have all contributed ideas that help our clients and that have made their way into this book.

I'd also like to thank Johanna Asher, my wife and chief of Speechworks operations. Johanna is my most valued source of counsel and has helped make dozens of decisions regarding this book and our company. Thanks also to Stephanie Frasier who runs our office. Stephanie is the true stalwart who keeps us all moving forward and on schedule. Without Stephanie's help in keeping our company running, it wouldn't have been possible to write this book.

Also, I'd like to thank Amy Collins MacGregor of The Cadence Group, who has managed the publication of this book. Her knowledge of the publishing industry, skill as an editor, and doggedness as a project manager have been invaluable.

Finally, I'd like to thank Spring Asher and Wickie Chambers, the founders of Speechworks. Spring and Wickie started helping our clients win business twenty-two years ago.

Joey Asher

Introduction

On a recent spring evening, I was with my wife walking our dog when my cell phone rang. When I saw who was calling, I took a deep breath before pressing the answer button.

"How did it go?" I asked, as I picked up, not even bothering to say "Hello."

It was the senior marketing officer of a large commercial contractor. We didn't need small talk. He knew what I wanted to know.

For the past two days, I worked with his team of experienced builders in a conference room. We hammered out and then rehearsed a new business pitch. The prize was a contract to build a $150 million office building. His was one of three firms on the short list. That morning, all three had delivered a ninety-minute pitch competing for the job.

"We won," he said, almost screaming into the phone. "They just called us to let us know. They said we blew the other teams away."

I did a little jig beside the road. My wife laughed. My dog barked. But I wasn't too surprised. I had seen the same thing happen over and over again.

My client had put together a great pitch with a laser-like focus on the client's key business challenges. The message was extremely simple and organized. They rehearsed it like crazy. They even spent a couple of hours going through all the possible questions they expected to receive. The team was prepared.

My experience has shown that with the proper preparation and planning, you can greatly increase your chance of winning a pitch.

That's what this book is about. You will learn how to consistently win new business pitches with a simple plan that applies to all businesses.

My firm has been helping companies win new business pitches for twenty-two years. We have worked with a broad cross-section of businesses: commercial contractors, law firms, architecture firms, accounting firms, insurance agencies, financial services firms, software firms, high-tech service providers, real estate firms, and many others.

We have helped our clients win billions of dollars worth of new business contracts. And we have learned that you don't win new business pitches by being the "best" firm. In fact, whether you are the best is usually irrelevant to whether you win.

That shouldn't be too surprising for most businesspeople. Generally, firms that make it to the short list for an important piece of new business do great work. And the buyer can't really tell which firm is the best. If they're honest, most competitors for new business would admit that their competition could also do a great job.

Since doing great work doesn't win the job, what does win? Repeatedly, we see that the firms consistently winning competitive business pitches are the ones simply delivering the best pitch. That means executing five simple sales pitch fundamentals better than the competition does. Those fundamentals include ensuring that the pitch is:

- Focused on a business solution
- Simply organized
- Delivered with passion
- Interactive
- Well-rehearsed

These five fundamentals are the ingredients for a simple plan to winning new business.

As you will see, this book is broken into five sections. Each section provides a detailed discussion and series of recipes for how to execute every step of the plan. You'll find stories taken from my experiences in helping my clients win new business presentations.

In working with dozens of companies across many types of business, I've found that all of them have one major thing in common. They worry about how to make their firm stand out from the competition. By executing the fundamentals in this book, you will stand out.

CHAPTER 1

Five Fundamentals That Distinguish Your Firm From the Competition

"How can we distinguish ourselves from the competition when what we are offering is so similar?"

That's the most common question my clients ask as they prepare to deliver a competitive sales pitch.

If you are on the "short-list" of firms pitching for a major piece of business, then you have established your firm as a qualified entrant. Distinguishing your firm from the other highly qualified firms is hard—especially in a short presentation.

Setting yourself apart from the competition crosses all industries.

For example, let's say you're one of three construction firms selected for the final round of pitches to build a new campus for a large insurance company. All of you have oodles of experience constructing similar buildings and could certainly do a great job with this latest opportunity. So how can you—in a forty-five-minute presentation—convince the owner to choose your firm?

Perhaps you're an architect. How do you distinguish yourself from the other short-listed designers when they've done just as many great designs as you and maybe even won more awards? During a one-hour presentation, you will all present photographs of beautifully designed buildings and discuss the efficiencies of each. How can you make your firm stand out?

Or say you developed a software solution to reduce costs associated with a client's accounting system. The competition, of course, claims similar capabilities. How can you make the prospect see that your solution is the best choice when you only have an hour to explain the complexities of your solution? And how can you even explain such complexities in that time frame?

Insurance agents, accountants, consultants, and every other industry have the same problem. All want to know how to make their firms stand out from the competition.

With this book, you will learn how to make your firm stand out from the competition and garner new business.

*   *   *

Over the past two decades, my company has helped clients win billions of dollars in new business contracts. We've worked with clients from a wide variety of industries such as construction, law, accounting, high-tech, insurance, financial services, and architecture.

We have learned that the best new business presentations don't focus on credentials. You simply can't "out-credential" your competition. The other guys are highly qualified too. They also have plenty of awards and great reputations, just as you do. Customers simply have no way of truly deciding who is most qualified.

Winning business in a competitive pitch scenario comes down to something simple: you must execute five sales presentation fundamentals better than your competition. These fundamentals, when done well, make your firm stand out in the eyes of the customer. They don't make your firm appear "the most qualified." Rather, these fundamentals make your firm stand out as the "best partner" for the job.

That's essential. You must connect with the buyer. These fundamentals will help the buyer think, "We like these people. They understand our problem. They seem like they're going to be a great partner on this project."

Here are the five fundamentals of a great sales pitch. The more effectively you execute these elements, the more you'll differentiate yourself from your competition.

FUNDAMENTAL #1: FOCUS THE MESSAGE ON THE BUSINESS PROBLEM

Many sales presentations begin with the firm's history or the speaker's experience. This approach is wrong.

Your listeners are not interested in your firm's history. And although your experience is important, it is not of *primary* importance. Your prospects are *primarily* interested in what you can do to help them solve their business problems. With that in mind, the best presentations propose a solution. Presenters can then weave in their relevant experience and credentials.

Proposing a solution usually takes a lot of legwork, research, and relationship building before the presentation. Although this can be very difficult, in the end it will pay off, as the best pitches propose solutions.

- *Less than a quarter of sales pitches propose serious solutions to the prospects' problems.*

- *This element alone will set you apart from three-quarters of your competitors.*

In coming pages, you will learn how to show up at the presentation with a winning solution that will excite your listeners.

FUNDAMENTAL #2: ORGANIZE THE MESSAGE AROUND THREE MEMORABLE POINTS

Most presentations are eminently forgettable. Literally. Usually, listeners can rarely repeat the core messages five minutes after the presentation. That's because the presentations are usually a jumbled mess with no clearly identifiable points.

Ask yourself this: What are the three things I want my listeners to remember at the end of this presentation?"

Make those points the focus of the presentation, using stories and other illustrations to bring them to life.

The goal is to create a simple, memorable message that will stick in the mind of the listeners.

- *Executing this element will separate you from 90% of your competition.*

This book will show you a simple, proven formula for organizing and focusing your message, a formula that has helped clients win billions of dollars worth of business.

FUNDAMENTAL #3: SHOW PASSION

I frequently see people pitch for huge projects while showing very little enthusiasm. Too many businesspeople speak with all the excitement of a houseplant.

Consider this. A vice president of construction for a large food company, whose job it was to sit in judgment of "bake off" presentations, says, "It's funny, but the final choice usually comes down to personal chemistry. We're looking for someone we like who seems enthusiastic about the work."

If you're hired, the prospect is going to have to spend a lot of time with you. With that in mind, they want to hire someone they like. Showing passion for their project is the first step toward building that relationship.

- *Few presenters speak with any real passion. This element will distinguish you from three-quarters or more of your competition.*

How you look and sound matters enormously. In all of these pitches, you are selling yourself. This book will show you how to present yourself in a way that is real and connected.

FUNDAMENTAL #4: INVOLVE YOUR AUDIENCE IN THE PRESENTATION

One of the best ways to ensure that you connect and bond with your prospect is to make your presentation interactive. So, turn your pitch into a conversation. If you're having a conversation, you're responding to your prospect's concerns. Hidden objections come out. You differentiate yourself by letting your prospect see how you solve problems and how well you understand their business. In short, you give your prospect insight into your intellect and empathy.

- *This single element will separate you from everyone else. By turning your presentation into a conversation, you are presenting yourself in a unique way. Whether that uniqueness is a good thing depends on your true qualifications and your skills as a presenter.*

This book will show you a series of innovative, interesting ways to engage your audience in a manner that makes them see you as a unique resource.

Fundamental #5: Rehearse...Rehearse... and Rehearse Again

Most presenters rehearse very little. Yet the people who listen to lots of business pitches tell me that in virtually every presentation they watch, they can tell who has practiced and who hasn't. Usually one firm comes across as substantially smoother than the rest. If you want to appear smooth and serious about getting the business, you'll rehearse.

- *Executing this element will separate you from two-thirds of your competition.*

Upcoming chapters will teach you the best way to prepare so that when the curtain goes up, you're ready to shine.

Executing These Fundamentals Will Win You Business

At the beginning of every football season, the great Green Bay Packers football coach, Vince Lombardi, would gather his players into a conference room. Walking into the room, he would hold up a ball and say, "Gentlemen, this is a football."

He would begin that way because he believed that to be great, you had to be great at fundamentals, and football fundamentals—like blocking and tackling—were the primary focus of the Packers' practices.

The same principle applies to every business pitch. If you execute the fundamentals well, you'll put yourself in the best position to win business.

Throughout this book, we will discuss the simple things that, if done well, will consistently make you stand out as clearly superior to your competition. Many of the examples focus on competitive presentation situations, the so-called "bake off" or "beauty con-test." But these principles apply to all sales presentations.

Simply put, this book is for anyone who wants to stand out from the competition and deliver business pitches that make money.

Fundamental #1:

Focus the Message on the Business Problem

CHAPTER 2

Present a Solution

The first fundamental of a great pitch is to focus the message on one thing: a solution to your prospect's business problem. Most sales presentations don't do that. Most sales presentations—the bad ones—focus on the speakers and their company.

"Thank you for inviting me to see you," begins the speaker. "Let's start by telling you a little about our firm."

Here's the problem: **NO ONE CARES!** What difference does it make that you have fifty offices worldwide? Does your prospect care if you have many big name clients? What difference does it make if you've won oodles of awards?

All the prospect really cares about is solving their business problem. The best presentations separate themselves from the competition by focusing on one thing: the business problem.

Why Should Your Pitch be Solution Oriented?

Question: Why is it so important to pitch a solution?
Answer: People buy solutions.

I'm not saying that people are only buying solutions in certain business situations. I'm saying that the only things people ever buy are solutions, regardless of the setting. It is essential to understand this if you want to learn how to win business pitches.

Let's say you're an associate in a hardware store that has begun carrying what you consider the best drill on the planet. It's the *SuperDrill 5000.* This drill is a super-duper hand-held model that comes with dozens of drill bits. The *SuperDrill 5000* is so light anyone can use it with ease. It's extremely powerful. It is fully portable and holds a charge for twice as long as the competition. And above all, it's absolutely beautiful. You've been selling drills for years and yet you actually get a slight thrill every time you look at the *SuperDrill 5000.*

Now, let's say that my wife walks into your store and is perusing the drills.

"Interested in a drill?" you ask.

"Yes," she says, "I need to drill a few holes for a doghouse I'm building for my dog Rocko."

"Have you thought about the *SuperDrill 5000*?" As you say the words, you feel that thrill of excitement. You think to yourself, "How could anyone not fall in love with the *SuperDrill 5000.*" Then you begin to describe all the features of the drill. My wife can hear your passion; she can see it in your eyes.

Then she points to another drill, the *K-250*—a lesser drill in every respect. "But this drill costs a third as much," she says.

You scoff at the *K-250,* reminding her of all the features of the *SuperDrill 5000*. "This drill comes complete with twenty-four drill bits. And it's so light."

"But I only need to drill four holes to make my doghouse," she responds. In the end, she goes with the lesser drill.

Why? Because my wife wasn't in the market for a drill. She was in the market for four inexpensive holes. Put another way, she had a problem. She needed a way to solve that problem. The *K-250* was the best solution.

Business buyers are just like my wife. They're not in the market for a law firm; they're in the market for a way to resolve a troublesome lawsuit. They're not in the market for an architect; they're in the market for a building that will help them operate more efficiently. They're not in the market for accounting software; they're in the market for a way to save money and streamline their business processes.

So, people buy solutions rather than companies—seems obvious. But many businesspeople don't get this point. Or at least they don't believe it enough to make it the focus of their pitches. For that reason, if you focus on selling a solution, you'll separate yourself from the competition.

And, more importantly, you'll grab your listeners' attention.

Let's look at this another way. Put yourself in the buyer's seat. A potential partner or vendor shows up to give you and your colleagues a presentation. They pull out their laptop, set up a projector, and say, "Thanks for having us in today."

Then they either:

A.   Talk about their company, the products and services they provide, how these products and services work, and how they are applied.

Or

B. Talk about several challenges you're very concerned about, then, tell you how they plan to eliminate or reduce problems associated with those challenges so that, in the end, your business will be more competitive.

Which presentation would you rather hear: the run-of-the-mill "this us what we do, what we make, how we make it, who we are, etc.," or the solution-oriented pitch?

Virtually everyone would rather hear the second presentation. It is immediately relevant to your life and business. It promises to help you with a real problem. It promises to help improve your business prospects and your life.

While writing this book, I interviewed many decision-makers and asked them why they make the decisions they do. They mentioned many things including price, expertise, industry knowledge, and relationship. Ultimately, however, decision-makers always come back to the need to find solutions to their problems.

I spoke with an in-house lawyer for a major staffing company and asked why he picks one lawyer over another. "We're looking for someone who understands our business and can help us manage our risk," he told me. In other words, he's looking for the lawyer who understands the business's challenges and can provide solutions.

Similarly, I asked a buyer at a major retail chain how he selects one vendor over another. "We're just looking for someone who can help us make money," he said. So if you want to win his business, show him that his stores' customers will want to buy your product and how much money he can expect to make.

If you ask decision-makers in virtually any industry why they choose the business partners they do, their response usually follows the "help me solve my problems" theme.

The Process of "Getting the Goods" Helps to Rig the Game

Grabbing your audience's attention isn't the only reason to focus your message on a business solution. The very process of identifying that solution—"getting the goods"—can rig the game in your favor. Why? Because the information-gathering process helps build the relationship that can help win the job once you reach the presentation stage.

Great salesmen at all levels understand the importance of *spending time* to learn about needs. One of my best friends is a star salesman for a major consulting firm. When he makes a sale, it's worth millions, but he started out selling shoes at Parisian in Birmingham, Alabama. He told me about how he used to sell shoes.

"When someone would come in to the shoe department, it would be my goal to have them try on as many shoes as possible," he said. "If they asked for a certain style, I'd bring out that style in two sizes. I'd also bring out some similar styles. I'd also bring out some outrageous styles."

"More than anything else," he explained, "I wanted them sitting there trying on lots of shoes for a long period of time."

"Why?" I asked.

"Because the more time they spent with me, the more they got to like me," he said. "Also, the more time they spent trying on shoes, the more invested they got in the process. All of that time made them more likely to buy shoes. It worked every time."

What does this have to do with winning a new business pitch? The same principle applies to selling anything. It is all about the process of gathering information to provide a true solution-oriented pitch.

To deliver a solution-oriented pitch, you're going to have to spend some time building a relationship with your prospect. At the very least, you're going to have to call them or meet with them to discuss their key business issues. In the best-case scenario, you would have been building the relationship for months, trying to understand your prospect's needs.

Most important, know that a great sales pitch doesn't stand alone. It is the culmination of a well-planned process in which you learn your prospect's needs and develop a relationship. That relationship gives you an important edge during the presentation.

Just like the shoe salesman, the more time your prospect has spent with you, the more likely he is to buy from you.

"Capabilities Presentations" Are Never as Good

Unfortunately, many people walk into a sales pitch without the goods or a solution to a business problem. This is likely because the seller has not done the homework or discovery required to understand the prospect's needs. The result: A presentation that doesn't address the prospect's needs and doesn't have as strong a chance of winning.

I was once hired by an architecture firm to help them win the contract to design a new headquarters for a well-known "big box" retailer. My first meeting was with one of the key architects who would be heading up the project if they won the job. In front of him, he had the request for proposals (RFP) from the retailer. We talked a little about the RFP.

At one point, I asked a simple question: "Why does this company need a new headquarters?"

The architect looked at me as if I had just asked him to solve a differential equation in his head. He knew the proposed size of the new headquarters. He knew the location. He knew that they had a "tight budget and schedule." The RFP had all that information—but the architect had no idea why the client wanted to build the building.

Why the client wanted the building is critical. Were they trying to build a showpiece to impress Wall Street? If so, then they might want a building that would garner publicity for its innovative style. Were they trying to develop a highly creative work environment? If so, then the building should be designed in a way that would bring workers together in exciting and creative work spaces.

This team of architects had not spoken to a single person from the prospect company. They had not attempted to scratch below the surface of the RFP to determine what the driving decision was to build a new headquarters. They had the specifications for the building, but they had no idea why this client wanted the building in the first place.

I helped this client as best I could, but I knew that they didn't have much of a chance to win because they knew nothing about the client's actual business needs. In the end, they gave a capabilities presentation, describing how they approach the building design process, introducing their team, showing other buildings they've done.

They spent in excess of $20,000 worth of time and materials responding to the RFP and putting together a gorgeous presentation. They had some of the most beautiful visuals you've ever seen. Their photos and drawings of other buildings were stunning. They talked about their many prestigious awards for their designs. Their lead designer was a guru for designing innovative office buildings. They showed more gorgeous pictures of those innovative buildings.

The problem, however, is that the other firms competing for the job could match their prestige. They also had gorgeous drawings. They also had won awards. They also had gurus.

What my client didn't have was the goods. They didn't understand the business problem the prospect faced. They lost to another firm that had the goods.

A Capabilities Presentation Is Really Little More than a Door-to-Door Pitch

A capabilities presentation is not much more sophisticated than the presentation Jimmy, our Fuller Brush guy, gave when I was a kid in the 1960s and '70s.

Every month or so, Jimmy would knock on our back door (I always wondered why he never went to the front door). We'd open the door and there would be Jimmy, an older, nicely dressed, balding man.

He'd say "Fuller Brush," and come in with his brown leather valise. He was a very nice fellow and my mom usually would offer him a Coca Cola or a glass of iced tea. If we had cookies, she'd offer him a cookie.

As he ate his cookie, Jimmy would open the valise and pull out his brushes. There would be floor scrubbing brushes, toilet bowl brushes, hairbrushes, etc. We would look and decide if we wanted any of it. We would have a nice chat about the weather or how the Atlanta Braves were doing. He would thank us for the cookies.

Ultimately, his sales pitch came down to this: "Do you need any of these brushes?" Sometimes we'd buy something. I remember my mom bought a toilet bowl brush from him, but most of the time, we would buy nothing. Jimmy would go away, only to come back again in a couple of months.

Most sales presentations today are nothing more than PowerPoint versions of Jimmy's Fuller Brush pitch. The seller gives no sense of understanding or caring about the customer needs. Rather, most presenters just present their wares and look at the client and say, "Do you need any of this?"

For example, I once worked with a software company that helped banks grow their automobile loan portfolio, often a very important part of a bank's revenue. The software was quite revolutionary in how easy it was to implement. Properly used, it could increase the number of auto loans the bank made.

This company was having trouble with its sales pitches, so they brought me a recent presentation. It was a forty-slide affair they had given recently to a bank that wanted to grow its portfolio of auto loans. The presentation apparently had not gone well.

And no wonder. It was little more than a capabilities presentation the sellers could deliver to all clients in exactly the same way.

The presentation had several parts, none of which addressed the bank's business needs. The presentation began with a history of the software company.

"Let's begin by telling you a little bit about us and how we got started," is literally how the presentation began.

Once the speaker got past the history of the company, he described what the software does in very technical terms. Apparently, the technology of this product is enough to make computer geeks want to take a cold shower. Maybe that's interesting to techies, but nothing in this part of the presentation addressed how they would help the bank get more auto loans.

Next, the presentation focused on the software company's revenues. There were charts showing the company's astonishing growth. I guess the point of these revenue charts was to show the client that they are a very successful software company. By this time, they were at least twenty minutes into the presentation, with nothing addressing how the software would help the bank grow its auto loan business.

The presentation then detailed all the software's features. There were quite a few slides touting features and benefits, highlighting how they had installed this software in many other banks. The final slide simply said "Any questions?"

Like Jimmy's Fuller Brush pitch, this software sales pitch utterly failed to address itself to the needs of the customer. To be sure, the software salesperson's wares were more complex than a line of Fuller Brushes, but the sales pitch did little more than open up a valise and pull out some stuff, show it off, and say, "Do you think you need any of this?"

Delivering a "Good" Capabilities Presentation

There may be times when you are just asked to give your prospect a sense of what you do. In this case, a type of capabilities presentation is appropriate.

So how do you do this? Talk about your business in terms of the solutions that you provide clients. Don't focus on your products.

I once worked with a software firm with dozens of information services products. The company's software could provide information for new employee and vendor background checks, information assessing the risk associated with insurance applicants, and identify prospects for new banking services. The firm also specialized in helping their clients re-engineer their information-gathering processes on new hires, insurance applicants, and banking customers.

It would have been a bad idea to list all of their products and the odd names. Instead, this company focused on their solutions. They identified themselves as a company that helps improve hiring processes, streamlines underwriting processes, helps lower risk, and helps banks lower their cost of customer acquisition. Instead of focusing on their products, they focused on the business solutions.

If you have to give a canned "capabilities presentation," at least make sure that it is solution-oriented.

A Solution-Oriented Pitch Provides Value before You're Hired

A solution-oriented pitch, under the best circumstances, sounds like an insightful, personalized business analysis that is highly valuable by itself. It's a free analysis of a business problem from someone who has spent some time really working on the problem. It's a presentation that demonstrates that you are well on your way to solving the problem.

Your presentation should be like the blue dumpster that a contractor left in my driveway one April afternoon.

Let me explain.

My wife and I were planning a major renovation for our house that included a new kitchen, master suite, deck, and driveway. We knew it was going to be expensive, so we obtained bids from three contractors. Mark was the highest bidder by about 5%. One day, I came home from work and in the corner of my driveway was a huge blue construction waste dumpster. I was stunned.

My wife didn't know anything about it. So, on a hunch, I called Mark and asked if he knew anything about it.

"I put it there," he told me.

"But we haven't selected you," I told him. "In fact you're higher than the other bidders."

"I suspected that we're higher," he said. "We're always a little higher. But I also know that you're interested in getting this project completed by the end of August before the kids go back to school. If you're going to do that, you're going to have to get started right away. I put the dumpster there so that as soon as you pick me, I'll be ready to start demolition right away."

"But we might not pick you, Mark," I said. "And if we don't, what happens with the dumpster?"

"I'll haul it away and pay for it myself," he said without hesitation. "I'm taking the entire risk there. I just want to get started. And if you pick me, I'm starting right away."

There are a couple of ways to look at this sales tactic. You might see this as a little sleazy. Perhaps he put the dumpster there to pressure us into picking him. I suspect that might have been part of the motivation.

However, my wife and I looked at it differently. We decided that Mark was showing us how badly he wanted the business by actually expending resources for our benefit before he actually had the job. We hired him.

What does all this have to do with creating and delivering a great sales pitch? A great pitch should be like the dumpster in the driveway. It should be a demonstration of how you have expended resources and begun solving your prospect's problem before they've actually hired you.

"Wow, these guys have begun solving my problem already."

Of course, just expending resources for your prospect isn't enough. You need to show that you understand your prospect's problems and that you've already spent resources trying to solve those problems.

The best pitches present solutions so detailed and compelling that they make the prospect think, "Wow, you guys have really thought through this problem and have come to us with some substantial work demonstrating your commitment to solve it." Get them thinking that way, and it becomes very hard to turn you down.

Here's an example. A large Washington law firm pitched for the chance to represent a major company as it was considering entering a bankruptcy reorganization.

Most law firm pitches are pathetic exercises in self-adulation. So, let me remind you, no one cares about your famous partners. No one cares if you have an office in Hong Kong. No one cares that you dominate your marketplace. All your prospect cares about is finding a solution to their problem.

And that's what this very prestigious Washington, D.C. firm kept in mind. They spent considerable associate and partner hours formulating a detailed plan for helping this company go into and emerge out of bankruptcy. The firm's senior partner told me, "We began the pitch by saying, 'We offer this plan knowing that you may not ultimately hire us. We simply ask that you agree to keep our proposal confidential.'" They knew they might be wasting their time. They knew that ultimately they couldn't ensure that their ideas were kept confidential, but they laid out their plan anyway.

Think about what happened. A big company is going into bankruptcy. They're wondering what will happen with their company. Are they going to survive? Are they going to be able to regain profitability? Will they have to be broken up and sold? They're scared.

Then a major law firm's senior bankruptcy lawyers put together a plan to help the firm successfully emerge from bankruptcy—before they are hired.

The lawyers spend several weeks putting this plan together, and base it on weeks of research and years of experience helping other firms emerge from similar challenges. This team of lawyers then walks into the pitch and simply lays out the plan, detailing exactly how they can help save the company. This is not a generic plan, but rather it's specific for this particular company. And it sounds good.

They were hired that day.

In a debriefing after the pitch, they learned that their competition had delivered standard "dog and pony show" presentations. None of the competition had offered anything more than elaborate capabilities presentations, discussing prior experience and resources. In other words, the winning firm's decision to use the pitch to detail a solution distinguished them from the other firms.

SOLUTION-ORIENTED PITCH MODEL: DEFINE THE PROBLEM, PROPOSE A SOLUTION

The model for a solution-oriented pitch is simple. You lay out the client's business problem as you understand it. Next, you lay out your solution. You might start your pitch by saying, "Based on our analysis, here is how we see your problem. We've done some work on this and we think we have a way to solve it."

Your solution should stand on its own as a valuable piece of consulting work. Just like Mark, our builder, you're putting a "dumpster" in the client's driveway. You don't spend any time talking about the history of your firm. You don't talk about how many offices you have worldwide. You don't talk about your revenues. No one other than your mother cares. (Does your mother even care?) You don't even talk about your credentials.

Instead, your credentials will be apparent as you talk about your solution and how you've implemented similar solutions for other clients. You focus your presentation solely on what the client really cares about—a solution to her business problem.

Solution Presentations Beat Capabilities Presentations Every Time

Let's look at an example of a presentation that did a nice job of laying out the problem and proposing a solution.

I was asked to help an architecture firm pitch for a chance to design a parking lot in a beloved public park. When I asked the lead architect about what the park was trying to accomplish with the parking lot, the architect was well-prepared because he had spoken extensively with the decision-makers in preparation for the pitch.

He knew that one key issue facing the decision-makers was not so much the design, but rather the overall viability of the project. They believed the park desperately needed parking, but they weren't sure the proposal would be approved in light of expected opposition from neighborhood groups and park supporters. The key issue was which firm could help push past the opposition and get the darned thing built.

This architect did a great job of "getting the goods." They did their homework and developed a pitch with more than just a plan for building a parking lot. The firm went in with a solution to the key problem, how they were going to shepherd it through the highly political and treacherous approval process.

They started their presentation with a description of how the proposed parking lot was garnering opposition from neighborhood groups. They then proposed a plan to successfully shepherd the project through opposition and finally get the lot built.

Next, they detailed their plan for approaching the neighborhood planning units and selling them on the project. They also related examples of how the same approach has worked to solve other clients' similar problems.

Of course, their presentation was right on target and won them the job, even though they had not been considered the leading candidate for the job when the process began. They won because they demonstrated that they understood the prospect's issue, and the resulting presentation focused squarely on providing a solution.

Don't Worry About Giving Your Solution Away

When I tell my clients that they need to detail their specific solution to the business problems in their presentation, many object and say, "That's giving away free advice."

My response is, "You give away the plan, but you charge them for the implementation."

Being stingy about giving away business analysis is shortsighted. I worked with a patent lawyer who had the opportunity to pitch for a significant piece of business. She received a detailed memorandum of the business challenge: help the company manage its patent portfolio better. She read the memorandum and went into the presentation prepared to show how she was qualified to handle the work.

She didn't win. When I asked her if she detailed her plan to help the company better manage its patent portfolio, she said, "No, I didn't want to give away free legal advice."

I responded as follows, "Have you ever given free legal advice to your housekeeper?"

"Of course," she responded.

"Have you ever given free legal advice to your brother-in-law?"

"Yes."

"And those people will never pay you," I said. "But you're unwilling to give away a little free legal advice to a company that could become a major, paying client? That seems a little silly."

"What if they take my ideas and then just go with our competitor?"

"That's a risk that you take," I said.

Indeed, it's a necessary risk. Your solution is what they're buying. They have a right to see it before they buy.

In the shaving business, it's an old adage that they give you the razor and sell you the blades. When you're determining what to say in your pitch, think the same way. The presentation should detail your solution. If they like what they hear, chances are they will pay you to make it happen.

CHAPTER 3

How to Get the Goods: Keys to Identifying Hot Buttons

If you've been paying attention, then you see how winning a pitch is more than just putting together a clever presentation. It's about putting together a careful analysis of the prospect's business needs. The next question then is this: How can you gather the needed information to provide a good analysis?

The answer: Use a consultative process. In other words, you need to talk to the prospect about their business prior to your pitch.

Salespeople who give great pitches think of it as the culmination of a consultation with the client. It's the icing on the cake.

First, you meet with the decision-maker, the potential users of the product, and other stakeholders. You listen to their needs and try to understand how you can use your resources to solve key problems they're facing in their business. Only *after* this "consultative process" do you then make a presentation.

Of course, many excellent books detail the consultative selling process. And if you want to be a great salesperson, you should make it your business to read many of them. I read a couple of new ones every year. I also go back and re-read my favorites, including *How I Raised Myself from Failure to Success in Selling* by Frank Bettger, and *Cold Calling Techniques (that Really Work)* by Stephan Schiffman.

They all have their own methods to approaching decision-makers—how to interview them, how to identify the key issues, how to be a good listener—and there are certainly variations in technique.

However, all consultative approaches ultimately come down to two steps:

Step 1: Listen for needs. Meet with the client and let her tell you "what keeps her awake at night." You're listening for key business problems that, if you can help solve them, will make you a valued business partner.

Step 2: Propose solutions. Once you understand the client's needs, then you propose solutions. That's consultative selling in a nutshell. The sales pitch is really the second half of that process, but you can't do a good job at Step 2 if you don't do a good job at Step 1.

Listen for Needs and Find Hot Buttons

To deliver successful presentations, you need to get the goods. You need to get your prospects to tell you their "hot buttons," their key needs that drive their decisions. That means you need to probe, ask open-ended questions, and listen.

Let's go back to Jimmy, the Fuller Brush man who would come to my house every few months. Imagine how it would have gone had Jimmy decided to use a classic consultative process, culminating with a sales pitch.

First, he would have called ahead and said something like this. "Mrs. Asher, it's Jimmy, the Fuller Brush guy."

"Hi, Jimmy. Are you coming by this month?"

"Actually, Mrs. Asher, when I come by, I'm not going to sell you anything. I'd just like to take about a fifteen-minute tour through your house with you, if that would be okay."

"Sure, Jimmy. But why?"

"Well, I usually bring you these brushes and just show you what we have, but I think I could be a lot more effective in helping you deal with your household challenges if I could just spend about fifteen minutes walking through your house. I won't charge you anything for my time. I just want the chance to really learn how I can help you best."

Jimmy then comes and tours the house, starting in the basement where he finds mildew in the corners where water has leaked in. Mrs. Asher explains that it always stinks in the basement because of that leak. Jimmy nods and takes notes. **One hot button obviously is to figure out a way to help with the basement.**

Upstairs, he sees that the boys' bathroom has a plunger that looks old and outdated.

"Mrs. Asher," Jimmy says. "I see that you have an old plunger there. Does it work?"

"It's funny that you mention it," Mrs. Asher responds. "We have that plunger up here, but it doesn't really work very well. Every time the toilet gets clogged, my boys have to call my husband, and he gets frustrated and calls the plumber."

"Does this toilet get clogged more than the other toilets?" he says.

"Actually, it does," says Mrs. Asher. "That's why the plunger is up here. The plumber says that the pipes up here are older and therefore smaller. That's why they get clogged."

Jimmy just nods and takes a few notes. **Another hot button is to help with the clogged toilet.**

Before he leaves, Jimmy looks at Mrs. Asher and says, "Thanks for having me in. I'm going to come back in two weeks and see if

I can't find a way to help you solve some of the challenges you're facing in this house."

"That's great," Mrs. Asher says, delighted.

When Jimmy returns, he's ready with a little presentation. He's going to propose some solutions to the challenges that he found.

"Mrs. Asher, when we took a tour of your house, I saw two major challenges," he begins. "Your basement has a bad odor because of a persistent leak, and your plunger doesn't really work. You also mentioned that the upstairs toilet gets clogged more than the rest."

Mrs. Asher smiles at Jimmy. She seems a little sweet on Jimmy.

"Now I'd like to talk about some solutions that we have for your household challenges. First, let's talk about the basement."

Jimmy proposes several things. A special brush used to clean mildew from cement. He also has a solution that can seal cement to keep water from flowing in the first place. Next, he offers a special super-duty plunger that has a bigger cup than the older models. He also has a special "home snake" that can be used to unclog toilets without calling a plumber.

Mrs. Asher buys all of it, but only after insisting that Jimmy sit down and have some milk and cookies.

Under this consultative approach, Jimmy makes a bigger sale. Rather than just showing up and displaying his wares, he's diagnosing a problem, and then proposing a solution. In the diagnostic process, he's also forming a much stronger relationship with his customer than he would have otherwise. So when he shows up for the final presentation, the decision-maker is predisposed toward Jimmy and his solution. "After all," thinks Mrs. Asher, "this fellow truly understands our challenges."

Just as Jimmy did in our little story, the best salespeople take the time to conduct some discovery to ensure they understand their clients' needs.

Apply the Consultative Lessons to Auto-Lending Software

In the case of the auto-lending software discussed earlier, how could we ensure that they're not just giving a "Fuller Brush" style presentation?

As previously mentioned, this software company helped banks grow their automobile loan portfolio. The software was quite revolutionary in how easy it was to implement. If used properly, it could really drive auto sales for the bank.

However, their presentations were nothing more than a forty-slide "Fuller Brush" pitch. They were essentially saying, "These are our products, do you want any of them?" As a result, they weren't having much success.

Like Jimmy, the discovery for this software firm should consist of trying to understand the bank's key challenges regarding the origination of auto loans. Perhaps the seller would learn that the bank has trouble selling cars because of poor relations with the auto dealers. If that's the case, then the presentation should focus on what her software does to improve bank-dealer relations.

Or, perhaps the seller would learn that the company wants to grow its auto loan portfolio by 50% over the next year. With that in mind, the pitch could focus on what kind of lending policies the bank should put in place when using the software to help achieve that fast growth.

The quality of the presentation hinges on how well you understand the needs of the client.

How to Get the Chance to Identify Hot Buttons: Ask

So how do you get the chance to find out a prospect's hot buttons?

Ideally, your relationship with the prospect goes deeper than just having been asked to submit a response to an RFP. You've known this prospect for years and have done other projects for them. You already have well-developed relationships with several of the key decision-makers. You've had many chances to study the prospect's business and learn the hot buttons. Ideally, you know their business so well that you already know what is driving the prospect's request when you come in and deliver a sales pitch.

Of course, we don't live in an ideal world. Many times, you deliver presentations for prospects that you don't know very well.

But that doesn't mean you have to go into the presentation cold.

My grandfather was a jeweler and a great salesman. He used to say, "If you don't ask, you don't get."

If you want the chance to conduct a discovery phase before you give a presentation, just ask for it.

Here's what you could say:

"We're looking forward to seeing you next week, and we appreciate you giving us an hour of your time. We believe our services can make a difference in your business. However, to make sure that our presentation shows you just how we can help, we'd like to spend a little time chatting with a few people at your firm before we come. Is that okay?"

It may not work every time, but generally, your prospect will let you chat with one, or several, of the key decision-makers. If they refuse, then you've done your best. More often than not, however, they will give you the time you are asking for.

How to Structure an Interview to Find Hot Buttons

Once you get the meeting and a chance to interview your prospect prior to the presentation, you have to decide what to say and do during the conversation. A conversation seeking to identify client needs should follow a simple plan.

First, you give the client a **meeting overview.** Schmooze briefly and then set the agenda. In setting the agenda, you want to give the client a brief overview of what your business does. After that, **probe with open-ended questions.** Ask the kind of questions that get the prospect expounding on his business.

START WITH A MEETING OVERVIEW

The goal of the overview is to take control of the meeting, give the prospect a brief overview of what your firm does, and demonstrate that you have a plan that will not waste the client's time.

Start with some light banter. "Is that a photograph of you and Tony Bennett?" Just don't go too far with the chit chat. A couple of minutes are fine, but too much schmoozing can be irritating, especially when you're taking up the prospect's time. Give the sense that you're there to find a way to help them. Redirect the conversation to the topic at hand: the prospect's needs.

Here's what you might say:

"Thank you for letting me meet with you. Our software firm helps banks build auto-loan portfolios. We do that with our software platform, as well as our consulting services. As I mentioned, we're giving you a presentation in a week or so, and we want to make sure that presentation is on target. So, if it's okay with you, I'd like to ask some questions."

You are accomplishing several things with this statement.

First, you're establishing that you're in control and the prospect doesn't have to worry about what to do during the meeting. This is important. Many sellers go into a sales meeting with no plan. Such a lack of direction is frustrating. It makes the prospect think, "I've given this person my time, and he has no idea what he's doing."

By clearly setting a direction for the meeting, you establish that you are a professional. "Hey, this guy has got his act together!"

thinks the prospect. In addition to relaxing the prospect, it also helps build the relationship. "Maybe," thinks the prospect, "he'll treat our business relationship with this level of professionalism."

Next, the meeting overview gives a brief "elevator pitch," which shows you're very customer focused. Keep the business description very brief and focused on its value to the user. This establishes that you're in the business of helping customers and that maybe you can help this particular prospect.

Finally, it's important to ask specifically for permission to go forward with the questioning. When the prospect understands that you want to ask questions that will help you help him, he will most likely say, "Sure, ask away!" He is now in the right mindset to tell you about his business. He knows that his job in this conversation is to give you information that will ultimately help him, and he's going to want to be forthcoming.

Probe with Open-Ended Questions – Mine the Gap

If you want to learn how to ask probing questions that help you win a pitch, it's helpful to understand what happens in the London subway.

In London's subways, there's often a gap between the platform and the train. Subway operators are apparently concerned that passengers will accidentally step into the gap and fall under the platform. To remind people of this danger, there's a recording of a lovely British woman constantly telling passengers to "Mind the gap."

Well, if I could play a recording during any sales call, it would say, "*Mine* the gap." What you're trying to do is find a gap between what the prospect has and what the prospect wants. When you find a gap, you want to figure out what is keeping the prospect from bridging the gap. That barrier is usually your prospect's hot button.

So the basic questioning pattern goes as follows:
1.   Where are you now?
2.   Where do you want to be?
3.   What's keeping you from getting there?

Where are you now? You want to explore their current solution and situation. What do they like about it? What don't they like about it? What are the challenges with the current solution? How did they select their current solution? What motivated them to choose that solution then? What has changed?

"So tell me what you're doing now to sell loans through auto dealerships?"

"How did you arrive at the current method for selling this way?"

"How does it work?"

"What are the challenges that the current solution presents?"

"How did you decide on that particular solution?"

"What were the key issues you were trying to address at the time you selected the last solution?"

Notice how these questions tend to be looking for a past factual assessment of the state of the world. These are great questions to warm up the interview with. They're usually easy to answer. They're not too probing. When you've asked enough of these questions, generally the prospect is willing to let you go to the next step in the diagnostic process.

Where do you want to be? The answer to this question is usually the major buying motive that will drive your presentation. You need to be able to say, "Your major business goal is _____. We're going to help you get there." The idea with this line of questioning is to get a sense of their ideal "end state." What is their dream? Ideally, you'd love them to say something like, "What we really want is _____. Can you help us get there?"

"So what are you trying to achieve with your auto loan portfolio?"
"Why is this goal so important?"
"Are there any larger business goals for the bank that this ties into?"
"Why is this your goal now?"

The answers to these questions are critical. They might say they're trying to grow their portfolio. They might say they're trying to reduce the risk associated with the portfolio. Who knows? But you need to know the answers. The answers to these questions are their major buying motive. If they say they're interested in growing their portfolio by 50% in the next five years, then the theme of your presentation should be, "We're going to show you a system that can substantially grow your auto loan portfolio."

What's keeping you from getting there? Here the goal is to explore what they believe is keeping them from achieving their dream. Getting at the seller's dream is a major key to being a great seller. People buy for their own reasons. And one thing most people in business will pay for is a path to their dream.

"What do you see as the key challenges standing in the way of your growing your auto loan portfolio?"
"What has made you focus on these particular challenges?"
"What have you tried to do to overcome these challenges?"

These questions give a fuller picture of what the prospect sees as the biggest barriers in solving its business problems. Perhaps the client thinks the biggest barrier to growing its auto loan portfolio is that the software systems that have linked them to dealers in the past have been too complicated and difficult to use. If that's the case, then you know that you have to emphasize the fact that your solution is not complex.

Many sales methods detail ways to organize your questioning during a sales interview. Most are too complicated for me. In my judgment, learning how to conduct a good sales meeting just takes experience. Fundamentally, you're just trying to discover where they are now, where they want to go, and what is keeping them from getting there. If you keep those goals in mind, you should be fine.

The biggest mistake most inexperienced sellers make is that they ask too *few* questions. With that in mind, here's a simple selling system that is a good guide:

"When in doubt, ask more questions. When not in doubt, ask more questions anyway."

I was working with a salesman who sold high-end enterprise software systems. We role-played an interview and I quickly mentioned that my company was having trouble getting the accounting software to link up properly with the software used by the marketing organization.

Rather than asking more questions, this new salesman immediately launched into his company's solution for the problem I had proposed. "Whoa," I said. "Be cool, dude!"

Just because you've heard a problem that you think you can solve doesn't mean it's time to start pitching your solution. Ask more questions! Think of the coaching that all good basketball coaches give beginning basketball teams: "Don't shoot before you make five passes." Similarly, I think you should never pitch before you ask ten questions.

NEVER PITCH BEFORE YOU ASK TEN QUESTIONS

Think of the questions that this seller could have asked. "What is the impact of this inability of the two systems to speak to each other?" "How does this problem manifest itself?" "What have you tried so far to deal with the problem?" And on and on.

The same is true for you. The more information you gather the better, and the decision-maker isn't going to pick another vendor while you're there in the room asking questions. So be cool. When in doubt, ask more questions. When not in doubt, ask more questions anyway.

Key Questions That You Should Ask

The numbers of questions you can ask leading up to a pitch are countless. But here are some good ones. Some may be more appropriate for your situation than others.

Ice-breaker questions
- How did you get into this business?
- Tell me about how business is going for your firm this year.
- How is the economy affecting your business?

Questions focusing on their current solution
- Who have you worked with in the past?
- What did you like about them?
- What didn't you like about them?
- What product have you used in the past?
- What did you like about the product?
- What did you dislike about the product?

Questions to understand the process for making the decision to hire a vendor
- Tell me about the process for hiring a vendor.
- Who are the key decision-makers on this deal?
- Tell me about their backgrounds, and what is important to them.

Questions focusing on what will motivate the current decision

- Why is this particular issue important to the firm?
- What do you see as the biggest challenge you're facing in this area?
- What do you see as the biggest challenge to achieving your business goals?
- Why are you seeking a solution to this problem now?
- What is your goal for this program?
- What would the ideal solution look like to you?
- How does this deal fit into your firm's business goals?
- How does this deal fit into your personal business goals?
- If this problem is solved, what is next for the business?

When in Doubt, Ask More Questions

A Couple of Lessons from My Grandmother and Basketball Coach Rick Pitino

One of my favorite sales sayings is, "No one ever listened their way out of a sale." Or put simply, "Shut up and listen." The basic idea for a business development interview is that the client should be talking, and you should be listening and taking notes. While there are many questioning methods sales books can teach you, ultimately, you just want to listen and let the client *kvetch*.

That's right, *kvetch*. For those of you who didn't have the benefit (as I did) of a grandmother who spoke Yiddish, to "*kvetch*" is to complain. You want to let your clients complain about what's bothering them. Once you get them *kvetching*, you just sit back and listen.

And no matter what, you must resist the overwhelming desire to present your solution. The goal here is to just listen and let the prospect's problems unfold in detail.

I once heard a story about how Rick Pitino, the basketball coach, became a great recruiter of high school athletes. Rather than going into the high school athlete's living room and talking about his school's benefits, he'd sit down with the athlete and ask something like, "So tell me what you're looking for in a college experience." The student would then tell him what was most important to him: education, a fun campus environment, a particular type of academic program. Based on those conversations, Pitino would then know how to position his college in the athlete's mind. It was by listening that he made the sale and became a successful recruiter.

The "Trial Close"

Don't try to sell the prospect anything in the first meeting. Remember, the object of your interview is to get ready for the pitch. If you try to pitch now, you might make the prospect think you're done and there is no reason for you to come back.

Instead, the closest you should get to pitching during your sales call is what is known as a "trial close." That's when you throw out possible solutions and see if they sound interesting.

A trial close might sound like this: "You mentioned that one of the challenges you're facing is how to get your software systems to speak to one another. I think we have some things that we can propose. If we could suggest something that would eliminate the need to re-enter data in the two systems, would that be something that you'd like?"

Then you sit back and listen again. As you listen, there is a good chance that the prospect will then elaborate on what he wants included in the proposed solution. "Yes, that would be great," the prospect might say. "But what we're also interested in is the ability to outsource some of this software management altogether. Is that something you can do?"

The trial close can work wonders. "We go back and forth with the management team and present solutions," said my friend the accounting software salesman. "We want senior management to get actively involved in our proposals. We suggest solutions and hope they push back and suggest alternatives. We want them to begin to visualize and live in our system. That's when we know we've made the connection."

When you have the prospect helping to create solutions in that way, you know you've "got 'em." Suddenly, the pitch starts to look less competitive. Suddenly, the pitch is a culmination of a process where together you've fashioned a solution. That's called "letting the prospect tell you what will sell them."

FINAL KEY TO IDENTIFY A HOT BUTTON

The most important key to identifying hot buttons is letting the prospect talk. If you let them talk long enough, eventually they're going to tell you the keys to making the sale. Of course, that also means you need to be listening. No one ever listened their way out of a sale.

If You Can't Get the "Scoop" Make Some Educated Guesses

I know what some of you are saying, "This is all very nice, Joey. But I live in the real world. We pitch whenever we get a chance. After all, like they say on the Lotto ads, "You gotta be in it to win it."

Okay. I know that many of you are going to pitch blind. Heck, I've done it myself.

Sometimes you just don't have the time to really delve into a client's business. Yet you want to pitch anyway.

But frankly, in today's world, there is little excuse for going into a presentation completely blind.

Every company has a website to give you a sense of their market. Public companies post annual reports and quarterly statements that, by law, include market analyses. Many public companies now provide audio and video of major presentations on their websites.

There are dozens of online information services such as Dunn & Bradstreet and Hoovers, that promise to provide you with information about your prospect companies. Just typing your prospect company's name into Google will usually yield more information than you can possibly process.

But there is another source of information that is often better than anything you can find online. It's your friends and colleagues. If you're with a company that has more than twenty employees, there's a good chance that someone in your firm knows someone who works at the prospect company.

In fact, several years ago, a software firm created quite a stir when it began selling a product that could scan a company's employees' computer databases for contacts. It worked like this. Let's say that you're about to deliver a pitch to Citigroup. And let's say that you want to know if anyone at your firm knows any key players at your prospect firm. You type "Citigroup" into the software program and it scans the Outlook contacts and stored e-mails for every employee in the company. It then generates a report telling you which employees have personal contacts there.

Many people felt that this software was an invasion of privacy. But the software company pointed out that if you're using your employer's computer to store personal information about friends, then your employer has a right to know that.

Regardless of what you think of the software, the point is that just asking around your office will likely generate contacts in your prospect company. Your colleagues should then be able to set up a conference call with their friends to discuss what they know about the prospect's key issues.

I'm always amazed at how easy it is to get good information from a prospect's company. I once was working with an attorney who badly wanted to get a meeting with the general counsel for a large paper manufacturer. "I don't have any contacts in the general counsel's office," he told me.

"Do you know anyone who works there at all?" I asked.

He shrugged and said, "Well there is one person, but she doesn't work in the GC's office."

"Who is that?"

"Well, my sister is a vice president of business development," he said.

I wanted to smack the guy in the head. "Call her!" I said.

Don't discount any possible content provider at a prospect's company. It often takes only a little effort to find someone who can give you the "inside scoop" on a company.

IF YOU HAVE NO GOOD INFORMATION, CONSIDER NOT GOING. IT IS VERY EXPENSIVE TO LOSE.

Why even bother pitching if you're not going to put yourself in the best possible position to win? It's a waste of time and money. With architecture firms, pitching for new business or responding to an RFP includes preparing drawings and charts, lots of staff hours and expenses. The total cost of a pitch can reach in excess of $50,000.

Many construction firms refuse to pitch when they're going in "cold," with no chance to visit the site or interview the key players. I once invited ten senior officers from commercial construction firms to a dinner to discuss their marketing practices. At one point during the event, I asked for a show of hands. "How many of you have been invited to pitch for opportunities based solely on your reputation or brand name?"

These were very well-respected firms, so all hands went up.

Here was my next question. "How many of you have actually won business in these 'cold pitch' situations?"

Not one of them had ever won in that situation. As a result, many stated that they had stopped responding to "cold RFPs."

I think you send a strong message to your prospect when you refuse to pitch without the opportunity to do some discovery. It says, "Hey, we're very serious about helping our clients. And we're not going to be able to truly help you if we don't get a chance to spend some time diagnosing your key challenges. We're not interested in working with anyone who is not interested in a true partnership."

That's exactly how an accounting salesman I know feels. He told me his firm is often invited to give competitive presentations. Whenever they are asked to pitch, he says, they ask for the opportunity to meet with the key stakeholders and analyze their needs. Sometimes they are asked to just come and give a presentation about their software's features, benefits, and price. "We say, 'no thanks,'" he told me. "We want to build a relationship. We don't sell software. We sell a solution."

When in Total Darkness, Guess

Finally, if you truly can't get any information on a company's true "hot buttons," we recommend that you guess.

That's right. Guess.

In my experience, people can usually make good guesses at what a prospect's needs are just by using a little common sense.

An architect I was working with was asked to pitch for a federal government building in Washington D.C. This architect was considered to be a highly creative designer, far more progressive than the other more conservative firms that had made the short list.

As is my usual practice, I asked the architects what they had learned from the decision-makers. "They didn't allow us to speak with them," the architect told me. "I guess they want to make sure that the process is completely fair. No bidder is allowed any unique access."

They were able to get a tour of the agency's existing space. It was a horribly designed bureaucratic-style layout with lots of unmarked doors opening off long, poorly lit hallways. "It looked almost like a Soviet bureaucracy," the architect told me.

Having taken a tour but unable to speak with the key decision-makers, the architects thought about what might be motivating the agency to invite such a highly creative architecture firm to pitch. They decided that the agency probably wanted a dramatic departure from the usual government style of architecture.

They went into the pitch with a series of "outside the box" ideas that would enhance the department's productivity and make it a fun place to work. The proposal distinguished them from the competition.

Often you will be able to guess at the key issues facing the prospect. If that's the case, then, by all means, do it.

There aren't many excuses for going into a pitch completely cold. With only a small amount of effort and resourcefulness, you will be able to get a good sense of what a prospect's hot buttons are. Then you'll be in a position to make a solution-oriented pitch that will always be better than a mere capabilities presentation.

What to Do When the Client Wants You to "Just Come and Tell Us About Your Company"?

Sometimes in a non-competitive situation, a prospective client will ask that you just come in to "tell us about your company." You should readily accept these types of risk-free invitations. Before you go, however, do everything you can to try to identify "hot buttons" and buying reasons.

How do you get the chance to learn what they need?

Once again, you can ask!

When they invite you to pitch, here's what you might say. "We're excited to come and pitch. In order to make sure that our presentation is on target and is as helpful as possible, we'd like to chat with you a little the week before. Are you available to chat on Tuesday?"

People want to hear useful presentations, so they'll often be happy to spend a little time chatting with you on the telephone.

Sometimes the prospect will respond, "Actually, we just want to hear what you have to say." When I hear things like that, I get nervous. In my experience, a refusal to truly engage you on their actual needs suggests a lack of serious interest on the part of the buyer.

If you're intent on showing up for the presentation anyway, it's best to view the meeting as a chance to start a relationship. Structure the presentation as more of an interview of the client, where you probe for their needs as much as you detail what you can do to help clients. How to create and deliver those types of presentations is covered at the end of Chapter 15.

CHAPTER 4

How to Win Without a Pitch: Be a Great Listener

Ironically, one of the biggest keys to delivering a winning pitch has nothing to do with your speaking ability. It has to do with your listening ability. Without a doubt, the most important skill you should develop as a seller is your skill as a listener. Your ultimate goal in sales is simply to let the **buyer tell you how to sell them**. You can only do that if you listen—really listen.

Great listeners get loads of business without having to participate in "bake offs," "beauty contests," and other competitive pitches. And when they do show up at the pitch, they win.

Why? They've built a strong relationship with the client by listening to their needs.

And while many sales books will incorporate a listening element into an overall system of asking questions, such systems are strained and hard to implement. Rather than focusing on how to put together the correct series of questions, I think great sellers need to make a lifelong study of what it takes to become a great listener.

Listening Helps you Identify the Key Buying Motive

To explain how listening helps you sell, consider the story of Dr. Ray Vaughn Pierce, who, more than 100 years ago, made a killing selling a "snake oil" called "Dr. Pierce's Golden Medical Discovery."

This elixir was supposed to cure everything from the common cold to a bad back to bunions. What I love about Dr. Pierce, however, was his sales technique. Before his "discovery" became a national sensation, he used to travel from town to town seeing patients. His "bedside manner" is worth noting by anyone who wants learn a thing or two about sales.

When he sat down with a patient, his conversation would go something like this:

"So tell me, where does it hurt?" he might say.

"Well, doc, my back is killing me," the patient might respond.

"Really, tell me about it."

"Well, I was at work the other day and reached down to pick up a box, and I lifted it up okay, but when I put it back down, I felt something twist."

"Really? How did it feel?"

"Actually, doc it really hurt, and it got worse as the day went on."

"Really? Tell me. At what point did it really get unbearable?"

"You know, doc, it really started bothering me at dinner. After I finished eating, I couldn't get up from my table. It hurt that bad."

"And tell me, how is it affecting your sleep?"

"Sleep? Well, doc, I'm having a lot of trouble sleeping. I toss and turn and I can't find a way to get comfortable."

[handwritten margin note: understand their P.O.V. and context of their decisions, problems, motivation, etc.]

"And how is it affecting your work?"

"Well, I'm not able to do any lifting. So they have me doing light work. Basically, my job is in jeopardy. If I can't get my back fixed, I'm in trouble. Is there anything you can do to help me, doc?"

"Well," Dr. Pierce might have said, "I think I have something that can help you. You mentioned that your back hurts and that you're also having trouble sleeping. I'm going to give you a case of something that specifically works with backaches. It's called 'Dr Pierce's Golden Medical Discovery.' Take it for six weeks and put lots of ice on your back. Do some stretches and you should be feeling much better."

And of course the patient would buy the cure. Dr. Pierce made lots of money with that approach to sales. By listening, he made the patients feel that he understood their problem and could cure it.

Consider how the conversation would have gone if Dr. Pierce, thirty seconds into the meeting had said, "I think I have something for you. Dr. Pierce's Golden Medical Discovery." He would have had far more difficulty convincing the patient that the good doctor truly understood the problem, thereby reducing his chances to sell the product.

In sales, the best salespeople adopt the same approach as Dr. Pierce. Great sellers know that it is extremely important to allow the prospect to spend time talking about their business. It allows the seller to truly understand the business. Just as important, the listening process allows the prospect to begin to *believe* that the seller understands his business.

"He must understand my business," the prospect thinks. "I've just spent several hours talking to him about it."

GREAT LISTENING IS ABOUT GIVING AND SOUL

So how do you become a great listener?

To me, being a great listener has a lot to do with personal generosity and soul. There are some jerks who weren't raised right and who just can't do it. Jerks don't tend to read books like this. So chances are you're not one of those jerks. However, if you are one and you're not willing to change, then you're probably not going to be much of a seller. Sorry.

Ultimately, listening is a selfless exercise. What you're doing is putting yourself into the mind of the person who is speaking. You're trying to understand. And at the risk of sounding rather "icky" in a business book, I think being a great listener is a holy thing.

I have an acronym that helps with listening skills. It's FACE.

- Focus
- Acknowledge
- Clarify
- Empathize

FOCUS

There is a scene in the movie *As Good As It Gets* when Carol the waitress (played by Helen Hunt), Melvin the bigoted writer (played by Jack Nicholson), and Simon the gay painter (played by Greg Kinnear) are riding in a car. They are going to help Simon ask his parents for money, because he's broke after having been beaten and robbed in his apartment.

Simon is about to tell about how his parents first found out that he was gay. Carol, who was driving, says the following. "Wait, I'm going to pull over because I want to give you my full attention."

That's the first part of great listening. You have to focus and give your speaker your full attention. That is not an easy thing to do.

First, there's a problem of simple physics. The brain can perceive in excess of 300 words a minute, but the average speaker speaks no faster than about 170 words a minute. So when you're

50

[handwritten margin note:] look away from computer, from pre call notes, wait for lull/pause to go back to notes for org./direction

listening, you actually don't have to use your full mental capacity to perceive the words. In other words, you have to focus to keep your mind from drifting.

And there's plenty of ways that your mind can drift. I believe there are three levels of focus.

Listening Level One: Hearing. You're actually listening to the person's words. That is, you're actually hearing everything that's being said, and you're not thinking about last night's episode of *Law and Order*.

Listening Level Two: Half-listening. You're listening, but you're also formulating your response at the same time. For example, the prospect may be telling you that they're concerned about how they can implement your proposed solution, and you're already formulating your response. By formulating your response before the speaker is done, you effectively miss the second half of his comment. There's an old joke that goes like this.

Fred: Hey Jack, what's the opposite of speaking?

Jack: I don't know, Fred. Is it listening?

Fred: No, Jack. It's waiting for your turn to speak.

Don't let that joke describe the way you listen. Don't listen to part of what the speaker says, begin to formulate your response, and just wait for your turn. You want to hear the whole thing before you start to formulate a response.

Listening Level Three: Active Listening. Here you're seeking to truly understand what your speaker is trying to get across to you. You're not judging the words as they come out; *no* thinking, "That's a stupid idea...I'm ready to respond." Instead, you're opening your mind and your heart to what you're hearing. You're just thinking to yourself, "This person's point of view is important. I think I can really learn something here. And I'm going to do everything in my power to understand." You ask yourself the question, "What is driving his perception here?" You listen for that, and if you don't hear it, you ask "What is driving that idea?"

Of course, some specific things can help you focus as you listen.

Dump Distractions

Turn off cell phones and pagers. If you really want to turn off a client, take a call on your cell phone during your meeting. I've actually seen this done. There's no greater insult. Taking a phone call during a meeting says, "I'm not sure who is calling, but there's a decent chance that he or she is more important than you." I would even go so far as to say that checking to see who is calling is an insult. When I leave my phone on by accident (and I've done it a couple of times, much to my embarrassment!) I quickly produce the phone and turn it off. As I do it, I make it clear that I'm not looking at who is calling. Saying, "I'm sorry," is also appropriate.

I know a business developer for a large law firm who often has clients in his office. When he meets with them, he makes sure his desk is completely clean—there's nothing on it, not even a paper clip. "I want to make sure that my client has the sense that there is nothing more important to me at this time than listening to them," he said. Clearing your desk helps the listener focus more as well.

Take Notes

I'm not a huge note taker. When I was in law school, I was the type who would take one or two pages of notes per lecture. One of my close friends took ten to fifteen pages of notes per lecture. I don't care how you take notes. But I do think that writing down what people say helps you listen better. You shouldn't, however, write so much that you never make eye contact with the speaker.

Pause to take notes – on phone, let "speaker" know you need just a moment to make sure you've captured it

BE CAREFUL OF PREJUDICE

Automobile salespeople will tell you that the biggest way to lose a sale is to prejudge the people who walk on to the lot. The scruffiest looking kid with the goofiest looking baseball cap may be a very rich rap star. Malcolm Gladwell, in his bestselling book *Blink*, interviewed a highly successful car salesman who said, "A green salesperson looks at a customer and says 'This person can't afford a car,' which is the worst thing you can do, because sometimes the most unlikely person is flush."

When you're listening to a prospect talk, you have to be aware of your own biases. The most unsophisticated sounding person might actually be quite a savvy customer. Don't let your own prejudices get in the way of hearing key information.

BE PATIENT

Sometimes, an important prospect will take too long to get to the point, or go off on ridiculous tangents. You might ask a simple question about who the key decision-makers are, and she'll start reeling off names that you know don't have anything to do with the decision-making process.

Or sometimes, the person you're interviewing will drone on and on like that boring teacher you had in high school. You might start to wonder where you left your *hari kari* blade, but you have to be patient and listen anyway. Sometimes that is the price you pay for the business.

Here's a test. What if I told you that you could get $10,000 if only you were to listen carefully to a really boring person? If that were the challenge, you would summon all your concentration and listen with all your care. Well that's the situation you face when you're listening to a boring prospect. Sure, she may be boring, but what she's telling you is probably worth more than $10,000 cash.

Ultimately, listening is a gift. It's a gift given unconditionally to the speaker. In other words, you don't get to say, "I'm going to listen to you, but only if you're not dull." If you're committed to being a great listener, you're committed to accepting the dullness with patience. Listening is about acceptance. It's about learning from the person speaking, regardless of how they speak. It's a holy thing.

ACKNOWLEDGE

Part of being a great listener is giving the person to whom you're speaking the sense that you're paying very close attention. This has to do with facial qualities. The best sellers and listeners have a great "listening face."

A perfect example is former President Jimmy Carter. No one has a better listening face than Carter. I met him in 1984 when I was a newspaper reporter. He had been out of office several years and was in Atlanta sponsoring a health care conference. In covering the story, I had the chance to interview Carter privately. He came into the interview room and sat down without the least pretense. I asked and he answered lots of questions. However, when the interview was completed, he didn't get up to leave. He started asking *me* questions.

"Where are you from?"

"How long have you been a reporter?"

"Where did you go to college?" And so on.

As I answered, Carter looked at me, smiled, and nodded. More than anything, I remember his eyes. They were big, blue, and crinkled a little at the edges. He seemed very interested in everything I was saying.

For the short time I was with him, Jimmy Carter, the former president of the United States, seemed fascinated with this cub reporter from the Gainesville, Georgia *Times*. To this day, no one can tell me anything negative about him. I love the guy. I've met many people who tell me that they've had similar experiences with Jimmy Carter. That is the power of a great listening face. It just makes people like you.

How do you show acknowledgement?

Eye contact: What your mother told you was right. You need to look people in the eye. For most people, eye contact isn't a problem. If you don't make good eye contact, then you have a serious problem that needs correction.

The CEO of a large medical software business once sent me one of his in-house lawyers for communication skills coaching. "He's a great lawyer," the CEO told me. "But he is ticking off everyone who works here. You need to help him with his communication skills."

When I met the lawyer, I did what I usually do when I work with people privately. We chatted. I had him tell me about his job and his communication challenges. Mainly, I just wanted a chance to observe how he communicates—to me.

Within fifteen minutes, the problem was apparent. He was a very articulate person. The problem was that when he spoke with you, he didn't make eye contact; rather, he would look up at the ceiling. As a result, he came across as arrogant.

I said, "Has any one ever told you that you make lousy eye contact when you speak to people?" He flushed a little and went silent.

"My wife," he admitted. "But I really never made the connection that it was a problem at work."

"You need to make better eye contact," I said. And that was all we worked on for the next hour or so. We had conversations in which I would catch him letting his eyes wander off, look up, or away.

It turned out that coaching was all he needed. He fixed his eye contact issue and kept his job.

Wives and husbands usually pick up on their spouse's key communication flaws. So here's some advice: if your wife tells you that you make lousy eye contact, listen to her! It could save you your job. More important, for the purpose of this book, it could help you make a big sale.

Animated facial energy. When someone is speaking to you, your face needs to indicate that you're paying close attention. Smiling and animated facial energy are the keys. Looking at a speaker with a blank face can hurt your relationship with a prospect.

During our workshops, we have an exercise that dramatically illustrates how facial energy can affect the person speaking to you. During this exercise, we pair participants into groups of two.

"One of you will be the speaker," we say. "The other will be the listener. The speaker will speak about her favorite food. The listener should make great eye contact. But keep your facial energy completely blank."

After having them speak for thirty seconds, we stop and ask the speakers how they felt. "I felt like I was speaking to a wall," is one common reaction. And indeed, speakers felt distressed in speaking to someone who gave such little facial energy.

We then do the exercise a second time, but after thirty seconds or so, we actually have the listeners switch their facial energy to become more animated. When we switch, the volume of sound in the room rises noticeably. The increased facial animation makes the speakers talk louder.

Great facial energy involves smiling at the speaker, nodding, wrinkling your eyebrows, shaking your head, and so on. You need to give the listener the sense that you're with them and that what they're saying is important to you.

Listen with your whole body. In addition to having a great listening face, great listeners also have great listening *bodies*. While you want to have lots of energy in your face when you listen, you want your body to stay relatively calm. A salesman called on me once and was the embodiment of poor listening style. He tried to sell me on a way to improve the number of hits we receive on our website. As I spoke, he had a blank expression on his face. As if that wasn't bad enough, he also constantly did a little trick with his pen, twirling it back and forth around his thumb. It was very distracting. He wasn't a great listener. In fact, he seemed almost distracted by our conversation. A great listening body gives the sense of being zoned in on the speaker. Your body and head lean slightly forward, showing your interest. Your head nods slightly. Your hands, however, are calm and distraction-free.

Verbal acknowledgment. When you're listening, give the speaker regular verbal acknowledgment. This simple thing can pay great dividends. Larry King, the television interviewer, once said that the two best questions he ever asks are "oh?" and "so?" Those little prompts can spur the speaker on and make them feel that you're really engaged.

Of course, a bunch of phony acknowledgements such as "Really?" and "Isn't that interesting?" won't cut it. You must be genuine. Another great television interviewer once said, "The secret to being interesting is to be interested." Again, that interest needs to be genuine.

But what if you're not genuinely interested? As paradoxical as this sounds, you should *fake the genuine interest.* Hear me out on this. William James, the pioneering psychologist, came up with the "act as if" idea. He pointed out that if you act a certain way, you will often begin to feel that way. I've found it to be true. For example, when my wife drags me to a party against my will, she will often say, "Act like you're having fun." When I do, I actually have fun.

If you act as though you're genuinely interested, chances are that you will be interested. When you're not interested in the person to whom you are listening, remember the words of French diplomat and writer Jean Giraudoux: "The secret of success is sincerity. Once you can fake that, you've got it made."

CLARIFY

[handwritten: Me! – understand first / solve /sell solution last]

Great listeners always ask clarifying questions. If someone uses a term you don't understand and it's throwing you off, interrupt and ask. "You just used the term 'facilities consultation.' I'm not sure what you mean by that." Some listeners will keep quiet out of fear of seeming ignorant.

Remember that the goal of listening is to truly understand; to learn from the person speaking. It's a selfless, holy act. If someone is using terms you don't understand, you're not accomplishing the goal of listening. You need to interrupt and ask for clarification. Your request for clarification proves that you're really paying attention and want to learn. The speaker feels complimented.

EMPATHIZE

Empathy means understanding more than just what the other person says. It means understanding how that person feels. True empathy is the ultimate goal of listening. To my mind, there are two ways to achieve a level of empathy with the speaker: take as much time as possible and ask them how they feel.

When you have a chance to sit down with a prospect, you always want to take as much time as you can reasonably get away with. Certainly, you don't want to take so much time that you're imposing, but the more time the better. Remember that the more time you spend, the greater the chance that they're going to tell you how they really feel about the matter at hand.

I recently met a corporate psychologist at a cocktail party, who gave me interesting insight into how to get at a person's real feelings. He told me that his job involved the psychological profiling of senior corporate executives. He made sure that people who were up for big corporate jobs weren't secret racists, sexists, or otherwise unsuitable as leaders.

"So what do you do?" I asked. "Give them some sort of test?"

"No, I just interview them," he said.

"That's all?" I said.

"That's all."

"And they just tell you if they're a racist?"

58

I was a little incredulous.

"Yes."

I was surprised. He explained that these interviews are long, sometimes lasting days. They will go over every aspect and incident in a job applicant's career. "So tell me about this incident that happened five years ago," the psychologist might say. And they will discuss it while the psychologist listens carefully.

"Eventually, you start to build a pretty good profile of the subject, including his attitudes toward minorities."

In other words, the key to really understanding how people feel is to take time.

This made sense to me, especially in light of my experience when I was a newspaper reporter. Good reporters learn that one key to getting a good interview is taking as much time as possible with the interviewee.

I learned the power of taking time with an interview early on in my career. When I was a reporter, I never allowed a source to speak to me "off the record." I didn't believe in it. So I began most interviews by warning the interviewee that "You shouldn't tell me anything you don't want to see in the newspaper. I don't go off the record."

And then I would try to get the interview to last as long as possible, asking question after question and letting them know how fascinated I was by everything they were saying. Inevitably, they would tell me things that they never really intended to tell a reporter. They would get so caught up in the interview that they would "let it all hang out." Sometimes, when they read the newspaper the next day, they were appalled.

"I didn't know you were going to put *all that* in the newspaper," they would tell me.

Listen for a long time and you will get more than just good information. You're going to get stuff that shows how they feel. That's what can win you the business.

(handwritten note in margin: "How do you feel about that?")

"How does that feel?"

Of course, very often, you won't be able to take too much time with a prospect. They have a business to run and will likely expect you to get your information quickly and move on. If that's the case, just be sure to ask the shrink's most famous and stereotyped question. "How does that make you feel?"

The great thing about sales is that there are no rules. And there are no rules about what you can and can't ask. If you want to know how they feel about their current software solution, then ask.

The same idea applies when you're trying to make a sale. Great sellers understand that the sales process takes time. The longer you spend with the customer, the deeper the relationship becomes. That relationship makes the customer more likely to want to buy from you.

The best way to deepen a relationship is to spend a lot of time listening to your prospect.

Listening is a Holy Thing

Great presenting starts with great listening. That's because you can't deliver a great presentation if you don't take the time to understand your prospect's needs. To be a great listener, you need to turn off your filters and your biases, and allow your prospect's feelings and information to flow over you. You need to take in and process everything they say.

Great listeners forget about themselves and immerse themselves into their prospect's world. That's what I mean when I say great listening is a gift and a selfless, holy act.

Chapter 5

Examples of Solution-Oriented Pitches

As you have learned, the point of the first fundamental is to set yourself apart with a client-focused presentation. It puts your offering in the context of the client's problem; it won't seem like "more of the same."

Let's end this section with a series of stories about how some of my clients have separated themselves from their competitors by digging hard to make their pitch as solution-oriented as possible.

Helping the Client with a Big Business Goal: The Insurance Broker Who Helped with a New Business Model

I worked with a large business insurance broker who put together a pitch for property insurance for a real estate company. The real estate company was bidding out its insurance to several vendors.

[handwritten annotations: "WHY?" "What is the trigger?" "motivation?"]

I asked the client, "What is the business reason for seeking a new insurance plan at this time?" Initially, no one knew and no one cared. "Look," I was told, "All of us have been given parameters for the coverage and we're all going to be providing the same types of coverage."

In other words, they bought into the idea that their business was a commodity. Let's be clear about something. Grain is a commodity. Soybeans are a commodity. Business services are never a commodity because the buyer sees their own problems as unique. Your job is to position your service as a solution to those problems.

Business Services are Never a Commodity Because Buyers See Their Own Problems as Unique

---

Companies always do things for larger business reasons. That includes bringing in potential vendors to deliver sales presentations. The firm that taps into that reason will go a long way toward distinguishing themselves from the competition.

After I insisted that my client explain to me the real estate company's decision to bring in a new broker, it turned out that they knew a great deal more about their client than they had initially indicated. The real estate company historically was a "management company." In other words, they managed real estate for other owners. But in the past few years, the company had changed its business model, becoming primarily a real estate *owner*, managing and operating its own properties. The decision to select a new insurance broker to manage the company's new level of risk was directly in line with this new business strategy.

It turned out that the prior commercial insurance broker was too small to conduct the heightened level of risk management services now needed. The real estate company needed an insurance broker to constantly evaluate their risk profile, ensuring that they were properly insured as their property portfolio changed. In other words, they needed a more sophisticated risk manager to ensure that at any given moment they had the lowest cost of risk possible.

All of this information didn't change the specifics of the insurance policies that would be offered to this real estate company. But it did make a huge difference in how my client positioned itself and its offering in their pitch.

know your audience

So how did all this make a difference in the pitch? With the key business goal in mind, the pitch strategy positioned them as the partner that could more effectively manage the real estate company's risk as they changed their business model and risk profile. Throughout the pitch, my client positioned itself as the team that understood the prospect's dynamic business needs, and was prepared to help them manage their risk and maximize their profits.

The notion that "In our business, everyone pretty much offers the same stuff" requires you to focus on the client's larger business needs. The goal is to distinguish your firm or business. To set yourself apart is to show you truly understand the client's needs.

SELLING THE RESULT: THE LITIGATORS WHO HELPED REDUCE BUSINESS EXPOSURE

Do you know the result the client wants? Can you deliver it? If the answer to both questions is yes, then, for goodness sake, tell them that you will deliver the results they are looking for.

At its highest levels, law practice is often referred to as a commodity business. All the big firms have excellent lawyers who know all the best tactics and strategies for doing deals and winning cases. But that doesn't mean that the buyers of legal services want a commoditized approach to their problems. I know a Fortune 500 company that conducted a "bake off" with four firms while seeking a law firm to litigate a major class-action race discrimination lawsuit.

ASM - I listened, I understood, I uncovered features they didn't know were available to them, re-evaluate their other vendors

According to the RFP, they were looking for a firm to help them win the lawsuit. The losing firms took the RFP at its face value. They assumed that the only "value" they were trying to serve was a victory in the lawsuit. With that in mind, they simply presented their qualifications. As it turned out, each was highly qualified to try the case; they wouldn't have been invited to pitch if they weren't. Their qualifications, however, did nothing to distinguish them.

The winning firm looked beyond the RFP to understand the lawsuit in a deeper way. They worked to understand the underlying business problems the company faced. They investigated the company's workplace practices, and then proposed a detailed strategy for winning the lawsuit. More importantly, by getting a clear understanding of the company's workplace practices, they were able to propose a plan to help change the internal practices that led to the lawsuit in the first place. All this positioned them as the clear winner.

The irony is that they were a small newcomer firm, not the entrenched incumbent that had done a great deal of work for the company in the past. The incumbent took the business for granted and they failed to deliver a differentiated pitch. They lost to the firm that distinguished itself by focusing on the prospect's problem.

Tying Your Service to the Business Plan: That's What this Builder Did

Virtually any business pitch can benefit from tying the service to the big picture needs of the decision-maker. Building owners typically do not look to construction firms to help them add to their bottom line. But that doesn't mean that showing an awareness of the owner's business needs won't yield nice benefits in a pitch.

I was working with a construction firm that was pitching for a chance to renovate a hospital. I asked, "Why do they want to renovate the hospital?" The contractor initially responded to my question with "Who cares. None of these guys expect a contractor to know that. They just want us to build a good building for them."

As usual, I persisted with my question. So, they made a few calls to their contacts and discovered the hospital was having trouble competing with a more modern hospital across town. Making the hospital a community showpiece and, ultimately, attracting business, was the reason behind the renovation. With that in mind, our presenters decided to open their presentation as follows:

> We know that you're interested in building a facility that will be the toast of your community and will help make yours the most state-of-the-art hospital in the community. If you hire us, we will deliver that kind of facility to you.

The rest of the pitch dealt directly with construction matters. But by opening with a focus on the hospital's big picture needs showed the owners that this was a construction firm that wanted to partner with them to help them achieve their goals. They separated themselves nicely from the competition by focusing on the business problem and won the job.

+ motivation

MAKING THE PROSPECT MORE COMPETITIVE: THIS SOFTWARE COMPANY HELPED INCREASE A BUSINESS'S PRODUCTIVITY

One of the best ways to win a pitch is to show how you can help the company make more money, spend less money, and generally become more competitive.

Here's a story about a software salesperson who did just that. Indeed, some of the best sales people I have ever met sell software. This particular accounting software salesperson told how a high-end mattress maker asked him to pitch against several of the top accounting software makers in the world.

"We spent six months trying to understand their business needs," he said. "They had multiple accounting systems, all relying on different information streams. The sales team had a different system than the accounting team, which had a different system from the distribution team, and so on. Everyone was working with different numbers."

As a result, no one was able to put together a complete, accurate financial picture of the company. They would plan to ship mattresses, but couldn't anticipate the numbers of pillows needed to stock as promotional items. "They were always reacting," the software salesman told me. "They were never proactive."

"We showed them how a fully integrated solution allowed them to anticipate and plan their business," he said. As a result, he said, "They bought our entire suite of software."

Give the Prospect a Taste for How the Engagement Will Progress: a Consultant Who Helped a Pharmaceutical Company Comply with a Court Order

Sometimes the key to winning is to simply detail your specific work plan for helping the client. This method will often separate you from the competition.

For example, federal regulators charged a well-known pharmaceutical company with over-aggressive marketing of a well-known drug. As part of the settlement, the company submitted to a Corporate Integrity Agreement, in which they agreed to hire an independent consultant to audit their marketing processes.

This was the first time the company had hired an outside auditor for this purpose and they had no idea how to go about it. They conducted a "beauty contest," bringing in several well-known firms and a smaller, but highly respected firm that was just getting into the business of auditing such agreements.

The smaller firm's presentation featured a comprehensive work plan, explaining exactly what they would do every week for the first two years of the engagement. They also included a detailed agenda of exactly what they would do on the first day of the engagement. Rather than just a proposal, they presented a full plan.

The pharmaceutical company could see that the smaller company had invested the time to really dig into exactly how they were going to help the pharmaceutical company through this.

Of course, the amount of work that went into the presentation was extensive. There were five presenters from the consulting company. Each of the five put in at least twenty-five hours of work. At a billing rate of $300 an hour, that came to approximately $38,000 worth of time invested in the process. "It's expensive," the managing partner told me, "but it's the only way to show that you really want the work."

As soon as they started talking about specific work plans, the tone of the presentation shifted. "At first it was like we were on opposite sides of the table," the managing partner told me. "But once we got into the details of exactly what we had planned for them, they started asking very specific questions. It almost became a work session. That's when I knew it was going well."

After the presentation, the drug company's general counsel, who was an integral part of the team selecting the consultant, said, "Let me tell you something, you blew us away. We haven't made a final decision yet. But I have a feeling that this thing is done. You will be hearing from us."

The presentation was obviously a huge hit. The consultant won the pitch, despite the fact that they were up against other firms with far better "brands" in the business. The managing partner told me that during a debriefing, they learned that none of the competitors did anything close to the amount of work. The competition's presentations included nothing but credentials. There was no analysis of how they would handle the specific auditing process.

 Bottom line: To separate yourself from the competition, you need to make your client see that you have a solution to their problem. This consultant understood that.

A Final Thought on Pitching Solutions to Business Problems

One of my favorite consultative selling stories involves Fred Herman, known as the "World's Greatest Sales Trainer." He appeared on *The Tonight Show* with Johnny Carson. Carson, in interviewing Herman, picked up the ashtray on his desk and asked, "If you're such a great salesman, why don't you try to sell me this ashtray?"

Herman took the ashtray and looked at it for a moment, turning it over in his hand. Then he looked at Carson and said, "Okay. If you were going to pay for this ashtray, what would you expect to pay for it?" Carson said he would pay ten cents.

Herman smiled at Carson and said, "Sold!"

Of course, Carson and the studio audience burst out laughing. But it was a wonderful sales moment. Herman knew that making a pitch is only a part of the sales process. Just as important is letting the buyer lead the process by telling what it will take to sell them.

Business people buy for their own reasons, not your reasons. And your job as a seller is to find out what those reasons are. You need to discover their hot buttons so you can hit on them during your presentation.

If the hospital building committee is worried that the cardiac wing they're building will disrupt the rest of the hospital, you need to know that so that you can address that issue in your presentation.

If the chief financial officer is frustrated that her current auditor's processes are too time-consuming for her staff, then you need to know that so that you can address how your approach will be less taxing on her resources.

Before you even think about putting together your PowerPoint presentation, you need to find out what is bothering the decision-maker so you can address it during your presentation. Hit the hot buttons during your presentation, and you will come out on top.

What is bothering the decision maker?

Fundamental #2:

Organize The Message Around Three Memorable Points

CHAPTER 6

Keeping Your Message Simple Separates You From Your Competition

If you've executed the first fundamental, you've done your homework and discovered your prospect's needs. You've identified hot buttons and business challenges, and you've come up with some ideas about how to solve the prospect's problems. Chances are that you've also already built a little bit of a relationship with your prospect as well.

That process of identifying and making sure that you're focusing on your prospect's problems will distinguish you from many of your competitors. Now it's time to create a presentation that's easy to follow and memorable.

To be clear and memorable, you must make no more than three major points. Why only three? Simply put, because people can't remember more than three points at a time. You can give them ten if you'd like. But they won't remember them. Give them three and you greatly increase your chance of getting your ideas to stick.

Why is it so important to keep your presentation simple and memorable with just three points? Because your competitors will consistently deliver presentations that are a disorganized mess. A three-point presentation makes you stand out as "the user-friendly option."

I once watched four construction firms pitch for a chance to build a new elementary school for a district in Boca Raton, Florida. All four presentations had *at least* ten points and were incomprehensibly convoluted. I had no idea what the main point of any of the presentations was. I can't believe that the members of the school board had any better clue.

If just one of those presentations had been simple and focused on just three key issues, it would have easily distinguished itself from the competition.

Don't Overload the Bridge: Stay within the Limits of the Medium

Organizing a simple message isn't that hard, but it does take discipline. When I ask my clients to tell me the three main points they want to make during a presentation, most can do it in just a few minutes.

If it's so easy, then why don't more people simplify their presentations? I think it's partly because most people don't understand that public speaking isn't a great medium for conveying lots of information.

Here's a story that illustrates the importance of keeping your message focused on a few key ideas. I call this story "How to Collapse the Bridge with Your Audience."

We have all seen road signs that say "Weight Limit 10 Tons." If you go on the Internet and Google the phrase "bridges with weight limits," you'll learn that every year dozens of bridges collapse because truckers ignore the weight limit signs. They see that the sign has a weight limit of ten tons. They know that they're in a twenty-ton rig. But they go across the bridge anyway, apparently thinking they can make it across before the bridge gives way. Of course, the bridge often collapses.

Most people fail to understand that the "public speaking medium"—the process of standing up and delivering information to listeners with words—is like a bridge with a weight limit. Only a certain amount of information can make it across the bridge to your listeners without a collapse in the communication process.

Presenters try to do too much, cramming too many ideas, facts, and explanations into their presentations. As a result, the presentations have little real impact. Listeners don't know what's important, so they forget most of it.

Fewer ideas mean a greater impact. Keep that in mind and you'll immediately improve the quality of your presentations, thereby rising above the competition.

YOUR LISTENER'S DISTRACTED MENTAL STATE DICTATES THE NEED FOR SIMPLICITY

Another way to think about the importance of keeping the message simple is to think about the mental state of your listeners as you deliver their presentations. With very few exceptions, here is the truth of their mental state: **They're usually not paying very close attention!**

Keeping your message to three points helps ensure that your audience gets your message in spite of their distracted state.
I will often ask clients to imagine how focused they are during a weekly episode of their favorite television program. Personally, my favorite show is *24* and if it's on, I won't let anyone bother me. I turn off the telephone ringer, and warn my kids not to bother me because "I'm watching my show."

I then ask my clients to compare that level of focus with how focused they are when they are preparing to listen to a typical PowerPoint presentation. Of course, the concentration level for a sales presentation is usually pretty low. Rarely have I heard anyone say, "I really can't wait to go to that presentation this afternoon."

The reason for such a lack of excitement is that most presentations stink. You should assume that when you get up to give your pitch, the overwhelming majority of presentations your listeners have sat through in their business lives have been dreary experiences.

They've endured rambling data dumps with no discernable point. They've suffered presentations with sixty-slides crammed into forty-five minutes. They've squinted at slides that are riddled with so many bullets that their eyes burn and their heads hurt. And just as terrible, the presentations are usually delivered by corporate drones who speak with all the energy of a potted plant.

Couple the traditional presentation quality with the fact that listening to business presentations—even in the rare circumstance when it's a good one—is never a leisure activity. People listen to presentations when they're conducting business. You're conducting your pitch while the listeners are also worried about a dozen other business problems, many of which may be more pressing than what you have to say.

So, when I say that the audience's mindset during a business pitch is "distracted," I am being generous. You need to assume that when you get up to speak, your listeners are often quite distracted.

By structuring your message simply, you will have a far greater chance of penetrating the fog. That, too, will separate you from your competition.

Chapter 7

A Formula for Creating Any Pitch

So how do we structure a three-point sales pitch that will hold the audience's attention from beginning to end?

We know that a good pitch presents a solution to a problem. To achieve this, follow a simple persuasive pattern —

"Problem/Solution/Ask."
1. Describe the problem as you understand it.
2. Propose your solution.
3. Ask for the order.

With this basic approach in mind, you can throw in many other things such as a description of the team that will be working on the project, your qualifications, etc.

This simple approach is counterintuitive for many businesspeople. Many businesses start their pitches by giving qualifications. But if you ask the people who watch these presentations, they'll tell you that they really aren't interested in hearing much about your credentials at the beginning of your presentation.

Here's an example of someone who did it right. A software salesman told me about selling distribution software to a major DVD player distributor. Their presentation had two parts: First, they described the problem, then they proposed a solution.

Their presentation started by pointing out how the manual processes in the prospect's warehouse were limiting its ability to grow, as well as leading to many shipping errors. "If you have people manually keying in invoices, that leads to the wrong goods getting shipped," the salesman explained to the distributor's top management. "It also means that they can't process as many goods as they could if this process was more automated."

The presentation went on to propose a solution. The speaker detailed exactly how they were going to eliminate their high rate of returned goods and how they could help them dramatically process more goods with fewer people. To be sure, they did tell stories of what they had done with other clients. But they only told stories of how they had helped other clients with similar problems. "One client reduced their return rate from twenty-five to one a day," he said. "Another client was able to increase their throughput at the distribution center by 50% with no increase in staff."

Those stories lent credibility to their claims that they could solve the prospect's problems. This DVD distributor had been very reluctant to upgrade to this new system. They initially felt that their current, although admittedly outdated, system was serving the business adequately. But they bought into the new software because the seller did such a good job of laying out a solution to their problem.

They won the business the way all great sales presentations

win business. They identified a problem, laid out a solution that persuaded the client to buy, and then asked for the order— Solution/Problem/Ask.

A Formula for Building Your Pitch

While the basic persuasive pattern for your presentation should be "Problem/Solution/Ask," you now need to know how to actually construct the presentation.

What exactly are you going to say? How much detail should you go into in describing the problem? How do you best outline your solution? How do you ask for the order at the end? More importantly, how do you do all of this in a way that is going to be memorable to your prospect? How can you do this all in a way that makes your presentation stick in your buyer's mind? Simple: You need a plan.

I base the formula for creating a successful presentation on the idea that impact comes from having a few tightly focused points, repeated three times.

Aristotle invented the idea that any presentation should have a beginning, a middle, and an end. In modern business presentations, this three-part approach translates to:

Tell 'em what you're going to tell 'em.
Tell 'em.
Tell 'em what you told 'em."

Another way to think of it is as a three-act play:

Act I is "tell 'em what you're going to tell 'em."
Act II is "tell 'em."
Act III is "tell 'em what you told 'em."

The ancient Greeks, in studying rhetoric, developed this idea because they understood that the spoken art is a limited medium, and if you want your ideas to "stick," you're going to need to repeat them.

Organize Your Message

So how do you present your business solution in a persuasive, memorable, and interesting manner? We recommend a simple three-act formula that tracks the Problem/Solution/Ask model.

Act I – Business Problem Overview/One Sentence Value Statement/Three-Point Preview

Business Problem Overview: Successful sales presentations start with a focus on the prospect's business problem. *"In speaking with the key stakeholders, we understand that your key challenge with this project is . . .*

One Sentence Value Statement: This simple statement lets the prospect know you have a solution that will help achieve his goals. *"In our presentation, we are going to lay out a plan to help you achieve your goal."*

Three-Point Preview: To keep the sales presentation memorable, stick with no more than three key messages. People simply won't remember more.

We will talk about three things today:
- How our program works
- How it will reduce your expenses
- How it will increase your revenue

Act II – Enhance Your Three Points with Stories and other "Evidence"

Break your presentation into three simple sections—the three key points. Illustrate the three points: describe your plans for the client, cite success stories, client testimonials, data, and other "evidence" that supports your proposed solution. *"This approach that we're laying out for you today is exactly what we did last year with ACME Corporation, when they had a problem similar to yours.*

Act III – Recap and Ask for the Order

To make your ideas stick, restate the core messages once again at the end. *"As we mentioned, we've talked about three things: How our program works, how it will reduce your expenses, and how it will increase your revenue."* After the recap, you ask for the order. *"We believe that the solution we've laid out for you today will save you hundreds of thousands of dollars a year and will make your business more competitive. With that in mind, we would propose that we move forward with a contract so we can begin helping your business as soon as possible. We want your business and want to get started."*

Over the years, I have used forms to help clients create their presentations. By filling out the following form, you'll have a good outline for your presentation.

PITCH FORM

ACT I: Tell 'em what you're going to tell 'em

Business Problem Overview: We understand that the key challenge you're facing is:

_____

_____

_____

_____

_____

_____

One Sentence Value Statement: We're going to lay out a plan to help you solve that problem and, more importantly, achieve your goals.

_____

_____

Preview: We're going to talk about three things today:

- Point one: _____
- Point two: _____
- Point three: _____

ACT II: Tell 'em

Point one: _____
Detailed evidence and information:

_____

_____

_____

_____

_____

Point two: _____
Detailed evidence and information:

_____

_____

_____

_____

_____

Point three: _____
Detailed evidence and information:

_____

_____

_____

_____

_____

_____

ACT III: Tell 'em what you told 'em

Restate the problem and recap the three points.
We've talked about how we can help you solve your key problem and achieve your key business objectives.

- Point one: _____
- Point two: _____
- Point three: _____

Ask for the order:

_____

_____

_____

_____

_____

_____

CHAPTER 8

How to Write Act I of Your Presentation

Let's dig into how you are going to create the first part of your presentation. This section of the pitch sets up the body of the presentation. Act I can often be the most difficult to create because it sets up everything else. It tells the entire story in a nutshell.

Remember that Act I has three parts:
- Business problem overview
- One sentence value statement
- Three-point preview

Business Problem Overview:
The problem overview seeks to grab the prospect's attention by focusing on something we know the prospect is interested in—the prospect and the prospect's problems.

Don't start with a discussion of yourself and your business.

"Thanks for having me here today. I'd like to start by giving you an overview of our business and how we've traditionally helped our clients . . ."

If you do that, you're wasting the moment when your listeners—distracted as they are already—are actually at their most attentive.

In studying attention spans, one social scientist determined that listeners pay the closest attention two to three minutes into a presentation. Their attention drops from there. By the fifteen-minute mark, most listeners' attention is virtually gone—unless you do something to revive the attention.

The point is that you need to begin fast, grabbing and keeping the listeners' attention early. And there's no better way to do that than by focusing on *the prospect.* With that in mind, the best way to open a sales presentation is to put the spotlight squarely on the main event of the presentation: the business problem at hand. No pussy-footing around. Let's dispense with the formalities and get to the good stuff. Start by describing what you see as the business problem that you plan to solve.

Here are a few examples:

- "We've been studying your company for the last six months and we see that the biggest challenge you're facing is an inability to get consistent accounting figures across your enterprise."

- "We know you're trying to build a showcase building that will be both a recruiting tool for new employees and a highly creative environment for fostering highly creative, engaged workers."

- "We know that the goal with this acquisition is to help move your business aggressively through the southwest, putting pressure on your rival and turning your organization into a true national chain."

- "We've been analyzing your current solution for the last two weeks. We think we can save you $500,000 over the next two years by switching to our product. And our quality is better than what you're using now."

If your presentation is going to be thirty minutes long, feel free to spend three or four minutes discussing the challenge or challenges that the company faces. Be as detailed as you like. Tell them about the work you did in determining their key business challenges.

"We have spent the last six weeks interviewing the top stakeholders in your organization about what they think of your current customer relationship management system. And here is what they told us . . ."

It's often a great idea to tell a story that illustrates their key challenge.

"We spent five days touring break rooms at your stores and found that not a single one had in place the most basic notices involving workplace safety. In fact, in one of your stores, we found fifteen workplace safety violations in plain sight in fifteen minutes. When we spoke with the store manager, she told us that there had been a minor workplace injury that very day."

Starting your presentation with this kind of laser-like focus on the client's business challenges, and your prospects won't be thinking, "Oh, this is just another boring PowerPoint presentation." Instead, their heads will nod in agreement. They will think, "These guys have really done their homework about us. I'm interested in hearing what they have to say."

Value Statement

The value statement is a simple statement that says you have a plan to solve their business problems and help them accomplish their business goals.

Here are some examples:

- "This presentation will detail how we plan to help you achieve your business goals and solve the problems you face in getting there."

- "This presentation is about our plan for helping you construct a building that will be a showpiece for your organization."

- "This presentation details our plans for how we can help you reduce your warehousing costs and help you make more money."

- "This presentation details exactly how we're going to guide you successfully through the bankruptcy proceeding that you face over the next year or so."

Although simple, the value statement is very important. This is the point in which you make it abundantly clear what you're going to do for the prospect; you're going to provide a solution to their business problem.

While you still have a long way to go with your presentation, such a statement gets you something very valuable: the prospect's attention.

Here's an example that shows how this method can hold your prospect's attention. Let's say you own a business and you're worried it is going to go bankrupt because of faulty accounting practices. Someone walks in, says that he understands your problem, and has a plan to solve it. What are you going to do next? Chances are, you're going to put down your BlackBerry, ask your assistant to hold all calls, turn off your cell phone, and pay attention!

The same thing will happen when you tell your prospect that you're going to solve their business problems. They may be skeptical, but they're going to tune in to hear you out. Suddenly, your presentation starts to seem qualitatively different from the verbal barrages they're used to sitting through. This presentation might change their life. And if they're thinking that, they are absolutely going to think that your message is better than the others. Now you're differentiating yourself.

Three-Point Preview

Most sales pitches don't have much structure. Sure, they'll have an "agenda" slide. But two slides later, the agenda has usually been abandoned for a loosely organized free-form presentation. You can distinguish yourself from the competition by organizing your thoughts around the three core messages.

Here are some examples:

Insurance Pitch
There are three core messages I'd like to focus on:
- Risk management policies and procedures to minimize your total cost of risk
- Implementation of your policies and procedures
- Monitoring your policies and procedures and adjusting our approach

Management Consultant

There are three core messages we're going to focus on during this presentation:

- Your automobile leasing process is costly
- How to re-engineer your process
- How to save $500,000 a year

Commercial Contractor

There are three core messages that we're going to focus on today:

- Our team can ensure no surprises
- Our communication plan quickly solves your problems
- Managing your site without business interruption

More Benefits of Focusing on Three Points

Of course, focusing on three points distinguishes you from your competition because their messages probably aren't so easy to follow. Three points also sets you apart by helping your audience remember your message.

A message that your audience can remember! Wow! What a concept!

Imagine that you're giving a presentation and I come up to you with a satchel of money. I say, "I'm going to give you this $300,000 if your presentation can pass a simple test. At the end of the presentation, I'm going to approach three listeners. I'm going to ask them to tell me the core messages of your presentation. If they can all give me the three core messages, then you will get the cash."

In that circumstance, what will you do? Almost certainly, you will limit your presentation to a few core messages, probably three. Moreover, you'll most likely remember to repeat the messages several times as a way of reinforcing your core ideas.

This "$300,000 challenge" is something you should strive to meet every time you give a presentation. Surely one test of a presentation's success is a simple, "What do prospects remember?" If people can't remember your core messages, then I would suggest that your presentation is a failure. You'll never pass the $300,000 challenge if you have more than three messages.

Getting down to three is not hard. Even a ten-year-old can do it. My daughter Annie was running for the position of secretary of the fifth grade class at her elementary school. She had written a short speech that she planned to deliver to the class the next day. When she asked me to read it, I failed to put on my "daddy" hat and proceeded to analyze her pitch as if she were the vice president of sales for a Fortune 100 company. She started crying and ran off to her room.

As all daddies with daughters know, nothing is worse than making your ten-year-old daughter cry. So I went to her room and tried a different, more diplomatic tactic. "Annie," I said. "Give me three short sentences on why people should vote for you."

Annie thought about it for a moment and then said, "I'm going to work hard. I'm going to listen to you, and I'm going to work to keep the bathrooms clean."

I then had her write three short paragraphs about each of her three key messages. Once she had done that, we added a short beginning and a short ending in which she asked for their vote. She did great and won her election.

The point is that coming up with three points is so easy that a ten-year-old can do it without much trouble. If Annie could do it so quickly, full-grown adults and business people should be able to do it too.

I worked with a management consultant who wanted me to help him pitch for an opportunity. He did a nice job of discovery and had a twelve-point plan for fixing his client's business.

"I think we need to get this presentation down to three core messages," I told him.

Nevertheless, he was stuck on his twelve-point plan. He had carefully worked out how, in twelve steps, he was going to improve the processes within the client's business and save them lots of money.

"But no one is going to remember twelve points," I told him. Indeed, people won't remember more than three of four points.

He claimed that it was just impossible to present fewer than twelve points. So I said, "Well, what if I took out a gun and threatened you? Could you get it to three in that case?"

"If you put it that way," he said, "I guess I could do it." We were able to distill his presentation to the three most important parts of his plan in no time at all.

Getting your presentation down to three points is not that hard and it allows you to have a huge impact on your audience. It allows you to be sure that they remember your message. That is critical if you want to win a pitch.

Keeping Your Message to Three Points is an Act of Leadership

Limiting your presentation to three core messages also makes you come across as a leader.

A sales pitch is ultimately an act of professional leadership. You're trying to lead and influence your prospects into buying into your ideas, but your listeners can't buy into your ideas if they can't remember what they are.

For some people, it's difficult to understand how speaking and presenting are acts of leadership. Just remember, as a speaker and leader, your job is to distill information into something simple that a listener can grasp.

One way to think of this is in the context of an oral argument in front of a judge in a courtroom.

For those who have not spent much time in the courtroom, an oral argument occurs when you go before a judge and make a verbal argument about a legal issue. For example, you might make a legal argument as to why a piece of evidence was obtained illegally. Here is how the process works: First, the lawyers write briefs laying out their arguments, and citing supportive cases and facts. The judge reads the briefs. Then the lawyers go in front of the judge and verbally argue the case.

But why is it necessary to make an *oral* argument? After all, the arguments were in the written briefs.

While the judge has read the briefs, he wants to hear from the lawyers as to what they think is most important. He wants to be led.

A sales pitch is just like an oral argument. As in court, you have often already submitted your written "arguments" before your pitch. Presumably, your prospects have already seen a proposal from you, have read your marketing materials, checked out your website, or examined your response to their RFP. They already have data about you and your capabilities. They also have data about your competitors.

As you walk in front of your prospect to give your pitch, your prospect, just like a judge, is thinking, "I know who you are. I've read your marketing materials and response to our RFP, but there's a lot of stuff there and it's not particularly clear to me. Just distill everything down to the key points."

Doing that for your listeners is an act of leadership. You're saying, "I've decided to tell you what is most important." To do that effectively, you need to be able to keep it simple. Most of your competition won't have the discipline or the courage to limit their message to a few points. If you do it, you'll stand out.

Make Your Three Points Listener-Focused

Remember that the first fundamental that distinguishes you from your competition is focus on listener needs. With that in mind, make sure that your three key messages focus on your prospect and your solutions to his business problems. If you're using the pronouns "you" and "your" a lot, chances are that you're doing a good job.

For example, good points sound like this:
- How your process is too costly
- How we're going to save you $100,000 a year
- How we can reduce your environmental risks
- How we can better manage your patent portfolio
- How we're going to increase your revenues
- How we're going to reduce your processing costs
- Our plan for your accounting process
- Our plan for lowering your construction costs

On the other hand, it's probably not a good sign if your points use the pronouns "our," "us," and "I."
- Our process for renovating an office building
- The history of our firm
- How we help our clients
- How we've become successful

All of these points focus on the speaker and her business, not on the prospect and your plans for helping them. Remember, no one cares about the history of your firm; no one cares about your process or how you help clients in a general sense. All they care about is how you're going to help them. Eliminate anything not focused on your listener's challenges from your presentation.

YOUR THREE POINTS SHOULD SOUND LIKE LISTENER-FOCUSED BUMPER STICKERS

So how do you actually phrase your three points? Think of them as "bumper stickers" that focus on customer value.

Each point should pass the "Johnny Cochran test." Most of us remember Johnny Cochran's famous line from the O.J. Simpson trial: "If it doesn't fit, you must acquit." That line was long enough to be substantive, yet short enough to be memorable. In other words, it was a bumper sticker. While your three points don't have to rhyme, they do need to be cohesive and easy enough to remember.

Let's look at the three points from the management consultant noted above.

- *Your automobile leasing process is costly*
- *How to re-engineer your process*
- *How to save $500,000 a year*

Each of these points is substantive, yet not too long. They could fit onto a bumper sticker.

Now let's look at how they might sound if they were too long.

- *Your automobile leasing process contains 50% too many steps largely due to the need to key in too many invoices.*
- *We'll re-engineer your process, eliminating three unneeded steps and reducing headcount by 25%.*
- *We'll save $500,000 a year through headcount reductions, and outsourcing of key steps.*

Each of these points certainly contains more information and is more thorough, but they are too long to be memorable. You won't get listeners to remember those three points through repetition.

On the other hand, let's look at the other extreme. How might they be too short?

Process
Re-engineering
Savings

The problem here is that they're more like subject headings than bumper stickers. As a result, they don't say much, which means there's not much your listeners are going to remember.

The Dangers of Being Too Clever

Often, presenters try to come up with three points that have a clever ring. My least favorites are the "Three Ps," "Three Cs," or "Three Whatevers." This attempt to give the presentation a clever ring seldom works. For example, a consultant's presentation might have been as follows:

Process
Pullback
Payback

My problem with the "Three Whatever" presentations is that they are usually too clever. Sure, they're cute, but do they really accomplish the goal of getting key messages fixed in the listener's brain? Would this consultant be satisfied if those were the only three messages that the listener retained? Probably not.

Other times, people will try very hard to make the bumper stickers themselves too clever.

Your Process is Fat
We're Going to Put It on a Diet
And You're Going to Lose Lots of Weight

Once again, this is all too cute. What you really want them to remember is that the process is too costly and that you've come up with a way to save a lot of money. The weight loss metaphor is clever, but once again, it clouds the picture.

Sometimes you need to sacrifice cuteness at the altar of clarity and simplicity. You're trying to win business here. You're not trying to win a poetry contest. Stick with a simple, easy to remember message.

CHAPTER 9

How to Write Act II: Stories and Other Evidence

If you've done a good job with Act I, Act II is usually easy. It's all about filling in the evidence of your presentation. The middle of your pitch provides the detail that brings the presentation to life. This is when you outline your plans for helping the client and provide evidence that proves you can deliver on those plans.

Here are a few examples of how you fill out the points of your presentation:

Insurance Pitch

Let's start with point 1.

- *We will put in place risk management policies and procedures to minimize total cost of risk.*
- *While this is a preliminary based on what we know about your business so far, here are some examples of the risk policies and procedures we initially have in mind for your organization.*

- *Let me tell you a story about how we used this same approach for another client just like you. [Relate a story about another client.]*
- *Just as that process worked for that client, we think this process, or something like it, will work well for you.*

Management Consultant
Let's start with point 1.
- *How your automobile leasing process is costly.*
- *We've spent the last two weeks going through your leasing process. If you look at your process, there are actually ten steps involved. We think that you can reduce the process to five steps with no loss of value to the customer or your organization.*
- *Specifically, we find that you're keying in the invoicing information at three separate times during the leasing process. That's wasteful. In fact, to run a test, we leased vehicles at three of your sites and here is what we found.*
- *By our estimation, your leasing costs are 25% higher than they should be.*
- *We saw the same problem with another of our clients. That client was Johnson Leasing. They had twenty steps, which we were able to reduce to five.*
- *We think we can do the same thing for you.*

Commercial Contractor
Let's start with point 1.
- *Our team is in a position to ensure that you have no surprises on this project.*
- *Let's look at our team. Our lead superintendent is Jimmy Franklyn. He has just finished working on a project very similar to yours. Here's what the VP for construction said about Jimmy and his performance on that project. "Jimmy*

*took care of us. We had some things go wrong on the project.
That's to be expected. But he always seemed to anticipate
what was going to happen. We were always in a position to
make quick decisions and move the project forward. We'd
build the next project with him without question."*
- *Your project manager is going to be Alan Williams . . .*
- *All of our team members have enough experience on this
type of project to anticipate the problems and therefore
ensure that you have no surprises.*

FILL OUT YOUR MESSAGE: POINT, PLAN, STORY

Let's look at this in another way. To fill out the key points for
your message: make your point, give your plan or analysis of their
problem, and then tell a story about how you have addressed this
similar problem successfully with another client.

Point:

As already discussed, your point should be simple and focused on
your prospect's business. It's a substantive bumper sticker.

Plan:

Deliver your plan or analysis with highly valuable content. The
idea is that the prospect should feel that they're very fortunate to
have you with them analyzing and discussing their business.

Story:

Tell a story that shows how this analysis or plan has benefited
other customers with similar challenges. End your story by
describing how you can apply the same solution to the prospect's
challenges.

Examples of the Point, Plan, Story Approach

Here are a couple of examples of how to execute the Point, Plan, Story approach.

Example 1

Point: *We plan to conduct a workplace safety audit.*

Plan: *Our plan for your audit includes three steps. First, we will review all of your safety records sorted by plant as a way of identifying where your safety problems are most pressing. Usually this process takes two weeks, assuming that we can get the records in a timely manner. Second, we will conduct detailed interviews of your employees.*

Story: *We conducted a similar safety audit for our customer Warehousing Incorporated. Just like you, OSHA sued them on numerous occasions for workplace safety violations. During the course of the audit, we were able to identify ten separate work processes that were ineffective and dangerous. For example, we learned that their workers were suffering a great deal of hand injuries while assembling their products. We identified a new type of rubberized work glove that will protect their hands while allowing the sensitivity and facility to allow them to work quickly and effectively. That single change reduced workplace injuries by 10%. We think we can get similar results for you.*

Example 2

Point: *Your manual data entry process is very costly.*

Plan: *Your manual data entry process, by our estimate, is costing you $100,000 a year. Currently, we see that you have three clerks entering the same figures into your system three times. One clerk is in the warehouse. Another clerk is in the main office. And a third clerk is in your sales office. The fact is that with the proper accounting package, you could eliminate the positions in the warehouse and the main office, and let the clerk in the sales office enter the data just one time. At $50,000 per year for each person, eliminating those two positions would save you $100,000 a year in costs.*

Story: *We worked with another retail client with a similarly costly manual entry process. We put a new process in place in which they only had to enter the data a single time. The process included re-engineering several aspects of their supply chain. It saved them $500,000 a year. We think we can get similar results for you.*

STORIES BRING YOUR SERVICE TO LIFE

I can't emphasize enough the importance of telling success stories in support of your plan.

More than anything else, success stories can give your prospect something that is very hard for them to get, a taste of the intangible thing that they're buying—a satisfactory result. Indeed, when people are buying things based on presentations, they're necessarily buying intangibles. (Otherwise, why would there be a presentation? No one buys a car based on a presentation. They just take a test drive.)

When someone hires a lawyer, they're trying to buy a result—a successful transaction or a win in a lawsuit. Those are intangibles. When someone hires a consultant, they're seeking to buy a reengineered process. That's an intangible. When someone hires a contractor, they're seeking to buy a successful project.

The problem, of course, is that it's very hard to look at the people making the presentation and guess who will do the best at delivering the desired result. Stories let the prospect see whether you've delivered similar results in the past.

Stories Eliminate Buying "Sight Unseen"

Think of it this way. Say you go into a jewelry store to buy diamond earrings. You describe the earrings you want while the jeweler listens carefully. He then says, "I think we have just what you want!" He disappears into the back of the store, only to return with one of those boxes that are just large enough for earrings.

He says, "I've got your earrings in here." Of course, you want to see them. But imagine what would happen if he said, "I'll only show them to you if you buy them from me." You would be incredulous.

Yet that happens in presentations every day. Business people deliver presentations without presenting solutions or telling success stories. In a sense, they're expecting people to make big decisions on solutions for their business without any sense of what the solution is or whether the team can execute. In a sense, those businesses are expecting their buyer to plunk down money for unseen diamonds.

But if you describe a proposed solution coupled with a story about how the same solution has worked elsewhere, you are helping the prospect see what they're buying. You want the prospect to say, "Oh, so that's how you plan to reduce my accounting costs. That's how you did it with a company just like mine!" In a sense, the plan, packaged with a story, is your way of showing the diamond in the box.

Stories De-Commoditize Your Business

The other thing stories do is distinguish you from the competition. The fact is that in many businesses, everyone proposes similar solutions.

I was working with an insurance executive who told me, "We're really not much different from the competition. We all offer the same risk management programs." When I spoke with the managing partner of a law firm, he told me almost the same thing about his business. "The practice of law has largely become a commodity business," he said. "The law doesn't change based on the firm."

Sure. Solutions, by themselves, can sound similar. But success stories are always unique. Sure, all law firms are going to propose similar strategies to win a lawsuit, but only you are going to be able to tell your story of how you won a similar case with a similar client in a similar industry. Your competition may be able to tell a story of its own (that is if your competition has read this book or has enough sense to tell its own success stories; and in our experience, most presentations fail to tell good success stories). Regardless, only you can tell your personal success stories.

Here's an example of how a story can really give the prospect a concrete sense of what they're buying. A construction firm was pitching for a major hospital renovation set in the middle of a bustling neighborhood. The hospital administrators wanted to be good neighbors and have as little impact as possible on the surrounding community.

In touring the site, the project superintendent noticed that one of the neighbors was a privately operated sleep clinic. To give the hospital administrators a sense of how the contractor would minimize the impact on the surrounding community, the project superintendent included the following as part of his presentation:

Point: *We know you want to minimize the impact on the local community. We certainly want to help you be good neighbors.*

Plan: *Our basic plan to help you accomplish this is to communicate with the neighbors, letting them know our schedule and working with them to have as little impact on them as possible.*

Story: *Let me give you an example of how this works. I notice you have a private sleep clinic adjacent to your site. We have worked near sleep clinics in the past. Of course, they do all of their work at night. So we meet with them to discuss our schedule. The last one we met with told us that they would prefer it if we didn't bring in materials after 10 pm at night. We learned, however, that we could bring in materials late at night on certain days. So we scheduled our late night deliveries on those days. We will work with your neighbors in the same way, seeking to accommodate them whenever possible. We're committed to having a strong relationship with the surrounding community.*

Analyzing this story, you can see that it does two things. First, it helps the prospect get a grip on the intangible thing that they're purchasing. In this case, the intangible is a considerate contractor who builds rather than damages relationships with the surrounding community. It would be easy for the contractor to just say, "We're going to communicate with the neighbors" and leave it at that. But that wouldn't do much in terms of really helping the prospect understand how they're going to get a good result. The sleep clinic story brings this intangible to life.

Of course, the story also separates this particular contractor from the competition. To be sure, all the contractors pitching for the hospital renovation talk about how they plan to be considerate of the neighbors, but only one could tell this story. Having such a story tells the prospect, "This is a contractor with a strong sense of exactly how to keep the neighbors happy." That works to help you rise above the competition.

STORIES HIGHLIGHT YOUR FIRM'S QUALIFICATIONS

Many presentations detail their credentials in a section titled "Credentials" or "Experience." As we have discussed, this approach does nothing to separate you from the competition. Replace your credential list with stories proving you've solved particular problems for your clients.

Success stories are the best way of credentialing yourself in a way that is relevant to the prospect. Tell how you've successfully solved problems for other clients that are similar to those faced by your prospect. Those successes demonstrate your qualifications in a relevant context.

Let's say you're a law firm trying to win the chance to represent an airline in a bankruptcy matter. You could start the presentation by listing all the bankruptcy proceedings you've handled, which is how many lawyers will start. "This shows our credentials," goes the rationale.

It's far more effective to start by saying, "Here is our strategy for your bankruptcy." Then lay the strategy out. Next, say, "We used this strategy when we represented Federated Airlines two years ago. In that case, we were able to help Federated emerge from bankruptcy two months ahead of schedule. We think we can get the same result for you." It's far stronger to put your credentials in a context relevant to the prospect's business challenge.

WHAT MAKES A STRONG SUCCESS STORY?

The best success stories are relevant and detailed.

The most important element for a good success story is the relevance to the prospect's business. You don't want to be deep into your story with your prospect thinking, "Why are they telling me this?" The "*Why do I care?*" issue is extremely important.

I once worked with an accounting firm pitching to a hospital. The firm wanted to tell a story about how one of the partners received great service from the hospital.

"What is the relevance of the story?" I asked.

"It shows that we patronize the hospital and that should help solidify the relationship," they answered.

A story merely showing a connection with the prospect doesn't mean much.

Also, you don't want to tell a story about the successful execution of a plan that has nothing to do with what you plan for the prospect. An example of an irrelevant story is that of a law firm describing successfully defending a products liability matter, when the pitch at hand is for a corporate contract dispute. "But it shows that we're great litigators," the lawyer might protest. So what! If you went in to buy a pair of sneakers and the clerk brought you a pair of boots saying "These fit about the same," you'd be unsatisfied.

Remember, the entire purpose of your presentation is to show that you can solve the *prospect's* business problems. Everything you tell them needs to be focused on *them*. In the case of the accounting firm, the only acceptable stories were those that were relevant to solving financial and accounting problems for other hospitals with similar challenges. For the law firm, the only relevant story would be one tied to resolving similar corporate contracts disputes. Everything else is a waste of time. Period.

In addition to being relevant, great stories contain details that add an air of authenticity. Consider the sleep clinic story: it's extremely important that the story was about a sleep clinic and not just some nearby business that operated at night. That detail added a degree of authenticity. It's also important that the managers of the sleep clinic didn't want materials brought in after "10 pm." Once again, the specificity of time lends an air of authenticity. Those details show that you were actually there. The listener is more likely to remember a detail like a "sleep clinic" than a more generic "nearby business."

BUT WHAT IF I DON'T HAVE A STORY THAT'S DIRECTLY RELEVANT TO THE PROSPECT'S PROBLEMS?

If you have no relevant experience at all, then you're in trouble. But it's my experience that most firms that make a short list usually have the relevant experience. If they can't find it, chances are they're not looking hard enough.

I know a contractor who pitched for the chance to build a new aquarium, although they had never built one before. Reasonably, they could have thought, "We have no relevant experience."

But this contractor had built many water treatment plants, which have many of the same construction issues as aquariums. The contractors used their water treatment plant experience as evidence of their ability to address aquarium issues.

They won the job.

If you don't think you have relevant stories to tell, go back and look some more. Chances are that they're there.

DRIVE YOUR MESSAGE HOME WITH A "POINT-STORY-POINT" SANDWICH

A common mistake people make when they tell a story is failing to drive home the point of the story.

Let's say you're an architect pitching for an opportunity. You know that one of the prospect's hot buttons is ensuring that the building is "green" or environmentally sensitive. Don't just start telling a story about how you've designed green buildings. Make a "point-story-point sandwich."

Start with the point. "Let me give you an example of how we've had success designing similar green buildings for other clients."

Tell the story. "Last year, a client came to us with a need similar to yours. They wanted to make sure their office building was a showpiece of 'green building' design." Blah, blah, blah.

Re-state the point. "That's an example of how we've been successful designing green buildings for other clients. We are going to do the same thing for you."

Making a "point-story-point sandwich" ensures that your audience understands why you're telling the story. That's important, because often the point gets lost. We often see presenters telling wonderful stories, but never explaining why the listeners should care.

"But if I'm telling a story about a green building, isn't it obvious that the point is that we're good at green buildings?"

No! It may be obvious to you. But that's because you're the one telling the story and it all seems so plain. You lived it. It's not obvious to your listener who doesn't know the context and didn't live it like you did. Remember that your audience is not carefully listening to every word. Their attention fades in and out. They may hear you talking about "green buildings," but not connect the idea that you're planning on implementing some of the same ideas into their building.

Also, it never hurts to drive home the point. The idea here is to connect with the listeners and help them. So be clear. Give them a "point-story-point sandwich."

OTHER FORMS OF EVIDENCE TO USE IN YOUR PITCH

Relevant success stories are by far the most important form of evidence used during a pitch. Nothing helps the prospect understand better what they're buying. However, you likely will want to use other forms of evidence, including testimonials, analogies, and data.

Testimonials are like stories. They rank close to stories in their persuasive value because they are a form of story.

Testimonials are best used as part of a story rather than alone.

Consider the same testimonial used two different ways. Choose which seems more persuasive.

Example 1: During the presentation, you read the following quote*: "Our experience working with Smith and Williams could not have been better. Their work on our distribution system saved us at least $500,000 last year." Jackie Anderson, CEO of Northwest Office Supplies.*

Example 2: During the presentation, you use the same quote in the context of a story: *"Last year we worked with Northwest Office Supplies, which had a warehouse distribution system just like yours. They too had to transport medium-sized goods from China through New Orleans for distribution throughout the Midwest. In analyzing their system, we found that their shipping costs were way out of line and they actually had overlapping distribution centers. Our recommendations saved them a lot of money. In fact, we told Jackie Anderson that we were pitching for this business and asked her if she would be willing to say something on our behalf. She readily agreed and said, 'Our experience working with Smith and Williams could not have been better. Their work on our distribution system saved us at least $500,000 last year.' "*

The second example is better, because the story gives context to the testimonial. Prospects are naturally skeptical of testimonials. We all know how these are manufactured. You call a friend who also happens to be a client and ask them for a favor. We see partial quotes from allegedly "rave" reviews in the movie pages all the time, and when we go to the movie, it stinks.

Telling the story behind the testimonial chips away at the skepticism. Take note of how in the second example, the speaker adds the story about how the quote was obtained. That's a nice touch. Once again, it adds an air of legitimacy to the testimonial.

Highly Persuasive Analogies Help with Complex Ideas

Analogies are persuasive and not used nearly enough. When you're trying to sell intangible services, analogies bring what the prospect is buying.

During the early years of the Internet boom, our firm worked with one of the early entrants into the Internet security field. At the time, businesses weren't aware of the dangers of hackers and computer viruses. So, to sell their services, one of their top executives came up with the following analogy.

Point: *We know you want to keep your network of computer data safe.*

Analogy: *We're going to install what amounts to a giant chain link fence around your company's data. We're going to have search lights going at all times to check for burglars. We're also going to have security guards checking the various entrance gates to ensure that no one is able to get into your system without your knowledge.*

Point: *That chain link fence will keep your data safe.*

That analogy sold many Internet security services. Why? When selling something complex such as Internet security services, much of your success depends on your ability to simply get your listener to understand what it is you sell. That ability is a very persuasive force in itself. The thought process is, "If he can explain that so simply, I guess he really knows what he's doing. I like that. I want to buy from him."

DATA MAY BE VALUABLE, BUT USE IT SPARINGLY

Another type of evidence you can use to support your presentation points is data, numbers, and other types of statistics. If you're going to use data in your presentation, remember this: It's a troublesome type of evidence for a pitch.

Spoken communication just doesn't "do" data very well and people don't find it very interesting. People don't generally look forward to PowerPoint slides with huge spreadsheets of numbers. Even "numbers people" don't care for such presentations. A CFO once gave me some great advice, "Most presentations that present data are terrible. I don't need you to review the numbers with me. I can read a spreadsheet without your help. What I want you to do is tell me what you think about the numbers. Tell me the most salient numbers. And tell me the stories behind those numbers."

With that in mind, we urge people to be very careful about how they use data in a presentation. Used well, data can get you hired on the spot. Used poorly, you're wasting your prospect's time and hurting your chances of being hired.

The most important rule about using data is that it be directly relevant to the prospect and his business. A common type of data that makes it into sales pitches is the seller's own sales figures. I worked with a software company that included, early on in the presentation, a very detailed chart showing the company's growth rate. "We've grown over 30% a year for the last seven years," the presenter would say. I guess the reason they cited this data was to show that they were successful and that the prospect should align itself with such a successful company.

So you're successful. You have the data to prove it. So what? Prospects generally don't care how much money you make. They care how much money *they* make. And if you're not telling your prospects how to make more money, then you're wasting their time.

If you're going to use data in the presentation, it should be about your *client's business* or *market*. If you really want to impress a client, come in with original data you've gathered about his specific business.

For example, a national operator of mall clothing stores wanted to hire a new marketing company. One marketing company in particular blew them away with their business pitch.

Here's what they did. Before the pitch, they asked for permission to visit stores and conduct customer surveys. After spending several weeks in the stores, they compiled customer data showing various fashion trends the retailer had never noticed. Within weeks, the retailer hired the marketing company to help create key marketing strategies.

Another way to impress a prospect is to deliver market trend data about the prospect's market. When I was practicing electric utility law (yes, it's as exciting as it sounds…), a management consulting firm called on one of our clients, a large utility company, seeking its business. A major part of the presentation was an analysis of where they saw the electric utility business heading at that time. They included trends for the prices of electricity, electric power plants, coal, and gas.

It was technical, but the utility executives ate it up because it gave insight into where their business might be heading. Once again, the key to using the data effectively was making sure it was extremely relevant and valuable to the prospect.

EVEN RELEVANT DATA CAN BE MISUSED

Of course, even if you have data that is highly relevant to your prospect's business, you can use it poorly. As I have said before, data doesn't fly through the air in a conference room well. People don't naturally relate to it as well as they relate to stories. So you need to be careful.

We tell clients to be careful when they select their data, when they present the numbers, and tell the stories behind the numbers. Most of all, interpret your data. Give your spin on what you think it means.

Let's go back to the fashion data presented by the marketing firm to the clothing retailer. The presenter had done an extensive survey of customer preferences with regard to women's dresses. The store was geared toward twenty-to-thirty-year-old women. However, the survey indicated that many women in their fifties and sixties were shopping there for themselves.

While the merchants knew that older women shopped at their stores, they didn't know to what extent. And the numbers were far greater than expected. They could have presented just the data and left it at that. But they did the right thing and presented more than the data. They told the story behind the data. They gave details of the interviews conducted with some of the older women who were choosing to shop at this store. The interviews gave interesting insight into the trends. For example, one of the women interviewed said that she had first become interested in the store when shopping with her daughter.

This interview told a story and shed light on the trend that the customer data alone could not. The marketing company, during its pitch, suggested that the retailer should consider special sales aimed at getting regular shoppers to buy gifts for their mothers. They also suggested that the retailer might want to find ways to capture more customer data about their customers' families.

This seller used the data successfully because they didn't just rely on numbers. The presenter also told the story behind the data, and then interpreted the data for the prospect.

Where do We Introduce the Members of the Team?

Business pitches often include a "description of the team." In fact, they're often required in architecture and construction pitches. The idea is that the prospect wants to get to know everyone who will be working on the project. We think that simply introducing the team members with no elaboration wastes a valuable opportunity to persuade. Don't just introduce the team. Show how each team member will help solve the prospect's challenges.

Usually the best place to put this part of the presentation is as part of one of the key points or after the value statement and preview, but before you start to detail the three points.

It should go something like this:

Architecture pitch
The three key things that we are going to talk about today are:
- *Our plans to ensure the building satisfies all your constituencies*
- *Our plans to give you flexible floor plans*
- *Our plans to bring creativity into the workplace*
Before we get into the details of our plans, let's take a moment and talk about the team members who will be working on the project.

When introducing the team, explain how each member fits into the solution you're proposing. Use the introduction as a way of reinforcing the three key messages that you're going to detail during the meat of the pitch.

For example, for the above architecture project, you might say something like this:

- *Our lead designer is Janet Williams. Janet has been designing flexible floor plans and creative workspaces for projects like yours for twenty-five years. We know flexibility is important to you and she will do a great job helping with that issue.*
- *Our project manager is Fred Jacobs. Fred will be the one conducting the on-site workshops to ensure that the building satisfies all the constituencies. He's worked with many companies that have complex constituencies. He's going to talk in a moment about his plans for satisfying all of your constituencies. We know satisfying all your constituencies is important to you and he will oversee that issue.*

Many presentations think of the "team introduction" slide as a throwaway. They just introduce the team and move on. That's a mistake. Use the introduction to show how the team is specially brought together to solve the client's business problems, once again separating yourself from your competition.

CHAPTER 10

How to Write Act III: Recap and Ask for the Order

Remember the $300,000 challenge? The one where I offer a presenter $300,000 cash if they can deliver a presentation that gets their listeners to remember the three key points?

Now is the time to make sure you collect your $300,000.

After you deliver the body of your presentation, it's time to recap your core points. Many presenters don't take this seriously. "The main event is over. Let's pack it in and get out of here," seems to be the attitude.

But the recap is a critical part of the presentation. It says, "These guys have their act together." It makes you look polished and it helps cement your key messages in your prospect's mind.

By now you realize that executing all of these parts of the presentation well will set you far above the competition.

That's because presentations are inherently messy things. If you're doing your job well, you're presenting in a fairly extemporaneous manner. Your prospect is interrupting you (if you're lucky and good), possibly sending you down a few blind alleys as you seek to answer incoming questions. That's why the recap is critical. It brings everything back around to the core message, giving your presentation a sense of cleanliness. It's a little flourish that puts a bow on your message and allows you to come across as professional.

Here is how a recap should sound.

Example:
You know we've touched on a lot of things. But I want to bring us back to what we see as the core message here. As I mentioned, our goal is to help you become more competitive by streamlining your automobile leasing process.

There are three core messages we've focused on during this presentation:
- *Your automobile leasing process is costly*
- *How to re-engineer your process*
- *How to save $500,000 a year*

Retelling your key messages has impact, and helps key messages stick in your listeners' minds. It's a way of ensuring that you don't just collect $300,000, but you walk away with the final prize.

Final Call to Action: Ask for the Order

At the end of your presentation, you need to ask for the order. My grandfather was a very successful jeweler in Hartford, Connecticut. He was a great salesman. He had many sayings about business success and sales. One of my favorites was, "If you don't ask, you don't get." With that in mind, it's very important to end your pitch by asking for what you want. You need to "ask for the order."

MOVING TO THE "NEXT STEP"

By "ask for the order," I mean that you need to ask the prospect to allow you to move to the next step in the sales cycle. The "ask" is especially important when the next step is not a final decision.

Indeed, the prospect doesn't necessarily know the next step in the cycle. It's your job to help by suggesting the next step and asking for action. If you're selling a software system, perhaps the next step is an analysis. If you're a labor lawyer, perhaps the next step is to get permission to do an audit of a particular labor practice. If you're an architect, the next step may be a "needs assessment."

Asking for the order is something that is very familiar to lawyers who make arguments to judges. When a lawyer makes an oral argument in court, one of the things that all good lawyers do is "ask for the desired relief." In other words, when you're finished making your argument to the judge, you're supposed to finish your argument with a clearly proposed direction for the judge. "Judge, we'd respectfully ask that you find for the plaintiff and direct the defendant to reimburse the plaintiff $100,000." Or, "Judge, we'd like to ask that you find for the defendant and dismiss the case with prejudice."

Asking the judge for relief gives the judge clarity on the next step and makes her job easier. Similarly, asking for the next step in the sales cycle gives the prospect clarity and makes her job easier.

All good pitches end by giving the prospect clear direction.

ASKING FOR A SALE: NO TRICKS—JUST PUT THE PROSPECT TO A DECISION

I was once meeting with a law firm managing partner. Toward the end of the conversation, he looked at me and got very serious. "I really just want you to address one thing in your program," he said. "I want you to address how to close a sale. We need closers."

The fact is that "closing" is overrated. Despite what some sales books say, there are no magic words to convince a person to buy from you. If you've proved that you can met their needs better than their other options, and they see value, then they will buy from you regardless of how you "close." If you haven't, they won't.

Of course, many salespeople continue to think there is some magic in the "close." I met a real estate salesman who swore to me that he closed many sales with the following technique. He placed a contract in front of his prospect and then proceeded to roll a pen down the table toward the customer. The idea behind this technique is that the prospect picks up the rolling pen to keep it from falling into his lap. Somehow, this salesman swore to me, this compels the prospect to sign merely because he has the pen in his hand. "That's called the 'rolling pen close,'" he said, appearing quite serious.

I had to suppress my laughter. Of course, these closing tricks are ridiculous. The best way to close a sale is to ask the prospect, gently, to make a decision. Here's a good way to do it:

We've laid out a way for you to save a lot of money. We think it makes sense. Does it make sense to you?

Your prospect can respond in two ways to this statement. Both of them are good.

First, they could say, "Yeah. It makes a lot of sense to us as well." Bingo! You've made a sale! Let's go get a contract and nail this puppy down.

Or, they can say something negative. "Well, I don't really think it will work." That response lets you know that you haven't made the sale. But this is good, too. Even if you haven't yet made the sale, at least you still have a chance to do something about it. Your response should be something that will tease out the prospect's key objection. "Really? Can you tell me where you think we've gone wrong?" And then, of course, you listen and hope that they will give you a chance to respond.

Now, the prospect could give a third response to the "does this make sense to you" question? They could give you a non-committal response. "Well, it all looks very interesting. Let us mull things over and get back to you."

In my mind, those "we'd like to think about it" responses usually are not a good sign. A non-committal "We'd like to mull it over" is generally a sign of a weak relationship with the prospect. If you've done your homework and really built a solution based on a true understanding of their business, then they should know you well enough to be honest with what they think of your proposal. Never forget that the pitch is the final stage of the presentation. If you've laid the foundation well, you'll reap the rewards with a candid conversation during the final presentation.

END WITH A FINAL COMMITMENT STATEMENT

I worked with a construction firm that had a simple rule for all of their new business pitches. At the very end of every pitch, the last person to speak would look at one or more of the key decision-makers and make what they called a "personal commitment statement."

We've laid out a plan for helping you build a hospital that will be a showpiece for your community. We think it's an excellent plan. But we also know that there are going to be problems and roadblocks that arise as we move forward with this plan. I want to tell you that my colleagues and I want this business. And we want to do a great job for you. And I promise that we are going to do whatever it takes to make you happy. We just want to get started.

I think that these commitment statements are very powerful for several reasons. First, they're rare. The idea of making such a bald, personal appeal is a little corny and old-fashioned. To me they sound like something you might hear on an episode of *Leave it to Beaver*.

"And Beaver, when you interview for the job, be sure to tell Mr. Crabtree that you promise to do an excellent job for him."

"Sure thing, Mom. Thanks for the tip." At which point Beaver will smile and give mom the "thumbs up."

Because they can sound a little corny, most people don't make those types of commitment statements. That is exactly why you should make them. No one else will. It differentiates you.

More important, I think you should make these commitment statements because they work. Commitment statements impress people if they seem genuine. People want to work with others who are passionate about their work, and who will do what it takes to succeed.

Finally, I think such statements are actually a compliment to your prospect. Put yourself in the buyer's shoes. Someone spent time examining your business and came up with a solution to a key business problem. Now they're looking you in the eye and telling you how badly they want to work with you, that they're committed to doing their best work for you, and that they want to get started right away. That prospect's thought process will be something like, "Wow, these people really are impressed with us and our organization and they really want to work with us. That makes me feel good."

Using The "Three-points" Formula When You are Forced to Use a Capabilities Presentation

Based on the first section of this book, you know that I'm not crazy about most capabilities presentations. In my mind, they rarely feel particularly relevant to the prospect. Most of the time, you can avoid these generic presentations. All it takes is a few telephone calls. "We're going to be taking up an hour of your time next week. Would it be okay if we spend ten minutes on the telephone right now to ensure that we can give you a presentation that you'll find particularly useful?" In my experience, most prospects will gladly chat with you about their needs if you ask.

Of course, I also know that in the real world, you're going to have to go into some prospects completely cold. One strategy for these types of presentations is to treat them as discovery sessions disguised as a sales pitch. We'll talk more about how to do that when we discuss interactive presentations.

But, as I have mentioned, the most important thing to remember when you're giving a pure capabilities presentation is to dress it up like a solution-focused pitch. Focus your three points on the solutions you provide to your clients, not the products you use to deliver those solutions.

For example, I worked with a large information services company that provides a background check service for its clients. Before businesses hire a new employee, they will run their information through this company's database to ensure that the new hire is not a terrorist or a murderer. It's a big and very competitive business.

If you're just giving your standard "dog and pony show," the tendency will be to simply list the various products you offer and what they do. The problem is that the product names often don't mean anything. The "Coverall System" will mean nothing to your prospect if they don't know more about it.

Instead, we recommend that you focus on the general benefits you offer your clients.

In the case of this information services company, they could focus on three key things:

- How we save our clients money
- How we reduce their risk
- How we can improve your systems

From there you can still use the Point, Plan, Story approach. For the first point, this client could say, "Let's talk about the process whereby we save our clients money. . . . Now let me give you an example of how this worked with another client."

While this presentation doesn't actually propose a solution for your prospect, at least it is solution oriented. It will most likely be far more interesting than a more traditional "capabilities presentation."

A Sample Presentation

So now let's put it all together. Below is a pitch I worked on in helping a large insurance broker win an opportunity to manage the risk of a real estate management firm. The prospect had been in the business of managing the real estate for others, but was in the process of changing its business model. Now, for the first time, the prospect was going to become primarily an *owner* of real estate.

The prospect's former insurance broker had primarily been in the business of finding the lowest rates. But now the prospect wanted a more sophisticated risk management program. That meant moving to a more sophisticated insurance broker.

Following is the script for the pitch that won them the business.

ACT I – PROBLEM OVERVIEW/ONE SENTENCE VALUE STATEMENT/THREE-POINT PREVIEW

Problem Overview: We understand that you have shifted your business to take on more risk of ownership, developing and owning approximately 80% of your buildings and managing only 20%. But as you take on more business risk, we also understand that you don't want to worry about catastrophic risk. You want to manage that risk more aggressively and in a more thorough manner. Ultimately, of course, the goal is to lower your total cost of risk.

One Sentence Value Statement: We're here today to discuss our plan for helping you reduce that total cost of risk in your business, thereby increasing your profit.

Three Point Preview: There are three parts to our plan.

- *Risk management policies and procedures to minimize your total cost of risk*
- *Implementing your policies and procedures*
- *Monitoring your program for effectiveness and adjusting where needed*

ACT II – DETAIL YOUR THREE POINTS WITH STORIES AND OTHER EVIDENCE

I.   First, let's talk about point one: Risk management policies and procedures to minimize total cost of risk.

   a.   This is a critical first step in minimizing your total cost of risk. It is our overall assessment of your risks. Think of it as a business plan to manage your risk.

b. The first step is to analyze your appetite for risk. Can you tolerate a lot of risk or not? We understand that you are willing to take on more risk as a way of lowering premiums.

    i. Of course, the problem is how to get your lenders to allow you to take on that larger amount of risk.

    ii. We will work with your lenders, educating them to help them see how their loan is not put at risk when you adopt a riskier profile.

    iii. How this has been done with other clients. Success story of working with other lenders to get them to buy into a riskier profile.

c. We'll also put in loss prevention procedures such as education programs about risks. Example.

d. Put in claims procedures. Right now your claims procedures actually end up costing you more money than they should. Example.

e. Reporting procedures. Example.

f. Publicity procedures. Example.

II. Second Point: Let's talk about how to implement those policies and procedures.

a. This is critical to minimizing your total cost of risk. The best business plan in the world is nothing without execution.

b. We train your managers in the entire claims process.

    i. What to do in case of loss.

    ii. How to report a loss.

    iii. How to mitigate a loss. Give example of how good training can minimize total cost of risk.

c. Execute loss prevention measures. Give examples of things that likely will be needed in this client's case.

    d. Give an example of an implementation for another client. Florida long-term care facility developer. Show how this client resembles that client.

III. Third point: Let's talk about monitoring the policies and procedures for effectiveness and adjusting as business needs change.

    a. Your business needs and risk profile will constantly change as you adapt to the market and enter new businesses. With that in mind, the only way to ensure that we minimize the total cost of risk is to constantly monitor and adjust our procedures and policies.

    b. Let me give you an example of how the business might change. What if you decide to develop in an earthquake zone? Here's what we might need to do…"

    c. Give example of how a developer client formed a construction firm. Suddenly their profile changed. But we adjusted their policies and procedures and were able to minimize their total cost of risk.

Soft Trial Close: We think this is a plan that will work for you. We're interested in what you think.

Act III – Recap and Ask for the Order

As I said, there are three parts to our plan.

- *Risk management policies and procedures to minimize total cost of risk*
- *Implementing those policies and procedures*
- *Monitoring for effectiveness and adjusting when needed*

Final Commitment and Ask for the Order: As your business moves into a new phase, it is critical that you minimize your risk of catastrophic loss. We can put a plan in place to ensure that you won't have to worry. We will minimize your total cost of risk and bring money to your bottom line. We're going to do everything in our power to ensure that you don't have to focus on risk management issues. Rather, we're going to help ensure that all you have to worry about is buying, developing, and managing real estate. We're ready to get started when you are.

Some Post Presentation Analysis

Act I – Problem Overview/One Sentence Value Statement/ Three-Point Preview

This presentation did what great pitches always do: put the prospect's "big picture" business problem front and center. The real estate company has just changed business plans and needs a more thorough assessment of its risk. Many insurance brokers will tell you that what they offer is a commoditized program of placing insurance with various insurance companies. Of course, that is true of many businesses. But the way to avoid the "commodity trap" is to remember that the prospect always thinks his business is unique and never sees his problems as commoditized. So if you start the presentation with a focus on the prospect, you'll never seem like a commodity.

Value Statement

I love value statements in which the seller promises the simple values the prospect wants. In this case, the prospect is simply looking to reduce the cost of risk and make more money. This value statement is a simple promise to provide a solution to that need.

Three-Point Preview

The great thing about these three points is that they totally focus on the plans to help the prospect. They constitute a three-point "elevator pitch" for the prospect's business. The pitch avoids the pitfall of telling the prospect about the seller. "Before we start, let me tell you about our company, our history, and our worldwide resources." This presentation avoids that recipe for boredom by clearly and simply laying out a proposed solution.

Three-Point Body of the Presentation

The way the pitch lays out the three points is a very nice use of the Point, Plan, Story approach to telling the story. The first point is that they plan to put together risk management policies and procedures to minimize risk. They then go into detail about what those plans include. Finally, they include examples of how this approach has worked with other similar companies. It's important to note that their success stories do not stand alone; rather they are in the context of the proposed solution to the prospect's business problem.

Once again, no one cares what you've done in the past, but they care very much care to see how your proposed solution for *their business* has worked for others. With that in mind, always put your success stories in the context of an example of how your proposed solution will work for them.

Soft Trial Close

Always ask the prospect what they think of your plan for them. Nothing bad can come of the response. Remember, if they tell you "it stinks," you're glad to know their thoughts. At least you can ask what specifically they don't like.

Recap

Most presentations underestimate the power of a good recap, but this presentation does not. By recapping the key messages, the presenters ensure the prospects remember the key messages. The simple recap gives a professional "finished" quality to the presentation. It makes the listeners think, "Wow, these guys have spent some time carefully thinking through exactly what they want to say."

A great recap simply and clearly repeats the most important key messages. You should not elaborate on the key messages. Just restate them.

Final Commitment and Call to Action
This presentation ends by emphasizing an eagerness to get started. I think that is one of the best ways to end a pitch. It tells the prospect that you love your work and that they're going to experience that love by hiring you.

Note also that the prospect has a nice little commitment statement. The seller tells the prospect that they're going to make risk management something that they won't have to worry about. Don't be afraid to make a personal commitment. It usually impresses the prospect.

Final Thoughts on Structure: The Five Commandments for Creating Your Pitch

Once, there were three guys going for a walk in the woods and they came across a bear. At first, they all froze in their tracks. They were terrified. But then they all tore off back down the trail. Suddenly, one of them stops, and pulls off his backpack and starts putting on his running sneakers.

"What are you doing?" his friends asked. "We can't stop! We have to outrun this bear!"

"Actually," he responded, as he laced up his shoes, "I don't have to outrun the bear. I just have to outrun you guys."

The same is true in competitive presentations. The goal is to "outrun" or distinguish yourself from your competition. With that in mind, when you get up to give a pitch, keep in mind that the vast majority of pitches that your prospects have heard in their business lives were terrible and hard to follow. That presents a great opportunity for the speaker who knows how to properly structure a presentation.

Most of the presentations that your prospects have heard have been rambling. They've been unfocused. They've had too many slides. They've centered more on the sellers' interests than on the needs of the prospects. They've included too few chances for the prospect to participate by asking questions.

But your presentation can stand out from the crowd by addressing those issues. Here are five commandments for structuring your message.

Commandment 1: Grab the prospect's attention and hold it by focusing on the prospect's sole interest: a solution to the prospect's business problem. If any part of your opening doesn't directly relate to making the prospect understand your solution to their problem, dump it.

Commandment 2: Keep the message focused by giving only three core points. Remember that speaking is a limited medium. The goal is to influence thought and action, not to unload a lot of data onto the prospect. Limiting your message to three core points ensures that you don't overload the prospect and that they will remember your key ideas.

Commandment 3: Preview and recap your message. Remember that you're telling a story of how you're going to solve the prospect's problems, and any good story has a beginning, a middle, and an end. The beginning should be a preview of your core points. The ending should be a recap of those core points.

Commandment 4: Help your prospect understand your proposed solution by telling stories of how you've executed the same plan for other clients. Stories are a very powerful way to get your prospect to remember your ideas.

Commandment 5: Make your pitch as interactive as possible. If someone wants to ask a question, stop your presentation immediately and answer it. Don't put it in the "parking lot" or otherwise avoid it. Questions are a golden gift. (Making your presentation interactive is the subject of Chapter 15.)

Follow these five commandments and you'll have the kinds of pitches that win lots of business.

CHAPTER 11

Visuals: How to Create Slides That Help You Win

The first thing you should know about your presentation slides is that they aren't going to win the job for you. Companies spend days creating PowerPoint slides for new business pitches. And yet so much of the time spent is wasted. Why? No one ever wins business with great PowerPoint.

Here are phrases I hear all the time:

- "We picked this team based on the fact that they seemed to really understand our business issues."

- "They seemed very well-prepared."

- "They seemed like a group that we'd like working with."

Here is a phrase I've never heard:

- "We picked them because they had really nice slides."

I have worked with many clients who present and win without slides. Presenting without slides allows you to focus on connecting with the prospect. On the other hand, I know it's impractical and often foolish to go to most presentations without slides. So here are some ideas on using slides effectively.

How PowerPoint Can Scuttle Your New Business Pitch

The first rule of using PowerPoint effectively is to make sure it doesn't cost you the job.

When PowerPoint turned twenty-years-old in 2007, I wrote a column that revisited a particularly gruesome scene from the sci-fi action film *Total Recall*, starring Arnold Schwarzenegger. In this scene, Arnold wraps a towel around his head and then sticks a metal probe up his own nose.

The probe then proceeds to crawl up into his brain and pull back through his left nostril a glowing red ball that looks way too big to make it out of his nose. Watching the ball slowly and painfully emerge, I cringed in my seat. As my ten-year-old daughter likes to say, "Now that's gotta hurt!"

The ball was a "bug" placed into Arnold's brain—sort of a human "Lo-Jack" that the bad guys secretly put there to track his movements. He had to get rid of it if he were going to save the country, planet, universe, etc.

American business needs a similar probe to remove PowerPoint from our collective corporate brain. I'm not saying that PowerPoint is evil. It's a fine piece of software for creating visuals to illustrate a presentation.

However, in some critical ways, PowerPoint has grown beyond an illustration tool and merged with our corporate presentation psyche in ways that hamper our ability to connect with clients and give good presentations.

Don't Use PowerPoint to Draft Presentations

First, the process of creating PowerPoint slides has merged in our corporate brain with the process of initially creating a presentation. As a result, we're creating terrible presentations.

Here's a scene that takes place thousands of times every day in businesses across America. Judy wants to create a new business pitch. So, she sits down at her desk and opens up PowerPoint and begins using the program's easy-to-use templates to outline her message. Before long, she has created thirty or forty slides, loaded with bullet points. She then goes in front of her prospect and narrates her presentation from the slides.

About two minutes into her speech, her listeners are busily thumbing their BlackBerries. Judy has bored her clients with too much detail and too many slides. Needless to say, the presentation won't be particularly persuasive.

Why?

In part, because PowerPoint encourages many bullet points and a boring outline format. We need to remember that PowerPoint is a program for creating visual aids, not drafting presentations.

Instead of turning so quickly to PowerPoint, Judy should have taken out a blank sheet of paper and written down three simple points she was trying to make to her prospect. She needs to focus on what the simple solution is that she proposes to the prospect's key business challenges. Then, she could use PowerPoint as a tool for bringing her ideas to life with graphic images.

PowerPoint Steals Rehearsal Time

Salespeople often spend so much time creating PowerPoint slides that they're failing to do the most important thing needed to give good presentations: rehearse.

Another way that PowerPoint harms presentations is simply by wasting time. It's a horrible time-suck.

I was on the telephone with an architect the other day who told me that they were consistently losing competitive presentations for new business. When I asked him how much time they spend rehearsing their presentations, he admitted that they didn't do much rehearsal. But after he e-mailed me their PowerPoint slides, it was clear they had spent several days creating gorgeous visuals.

Let's be clear about something. If it comes down to a choice between PowerPoint and rehearsal, dump the slides. For a thirty-minute presentation, use eight to ten slides at the most. Save your time for rehearsal.

Plenty of people are great presenters without PowerPoint. No one is great without rehearsal.

The Tribble with Slides: They Can Overpower Your Presentation

Another way PowerPoint scuttles presentations is by over-whelming them. One of my favorite *Star Trek* episodes is the "The Trouble with Tribbles." That's the one where Lt. Uhura brings to the ship a cute little furry creature known as a "tribble." The tribbles are cute, about the size of a guinea pig, and coo in a very endearing way when you pet them. They're very lovable.

The trouble with tribbles is that they reproduce at a rate that literally takes over the ship, making it hard to move and threatening the safety of the passengers. In fact, the episode ends when Scotty, the engineer, saves the day by beaming them aboard the enemy Klingon vessel.

Slides are like tribbles. A few of them are fine. The problem is that many presenters tend to become so enchanted with them, that they take over the presentation. Indeed, too many slides will literally kill your presentation and scuttle your chance of winning the pitch.

That's because the most important visuals in the room are the presenters. You want the prospect looking at you and your colleagues, not the slides. You want them engaging with you, discussing the issues around their project. You don't want them sitting in the dark, listening while you say things like, "On this next slide . . ."

When you create your slides, remember that you want to make the prospect believe that you and your colleagues are the ones they should trust to solve their business problem. If all you do is narrate slides and never connect with your audience, you will fail. You will never be able to engage your prospect in a personal way. You will never be able to let them look you in the eye and get a feel for something that is very important: whether they like you.

So be careful with your slides! Don't overwhelm your presentation with slides. Don't turn your presentation into a slide show in which you're narrating fifty slides in a thirty-minute time frame. If you do that, your slides have become tribbles. The problem is that you won't have Scotty to bail you out before your ship goes down.

How to Create Effective PowerPoint Slides: Begin by Understanding Them

How can you use slides without them upstaging you? The most important thing is to grasp the essence of the slide. In other words, what are slides good for?

Most simply, they're good for showing stuff that can't be detailed simply in words. They're also good for reinforcing your key messages.

Your core ideas on an agenda slide: If you're following the method detailed in this book, then you're going to want your prospect to remember a few core ideas. Create a single slide that puts those ideas in one place. The agenda slide should come early in your presentation. For example:

Agenda

- Your automobile leasing process is costly
- How to re-engineer your process
- How to save $500,000 a year

Photographs or drawings of relevant creations: Mock-ups and drawings of your proposed ideas are certainly important, especially in construction, engineering, and architectural presentations. If you've done initial drawings of a new building you are going to construct, you certainly want to show them. If you're an architect who is going to design a large building, you certainly want to show photographs of buildings you've designed in the past that are similar to the one that you will design for the prospect.

Complicated processes: If you want your prospect to understand the complicated way you're going to reform their supply chain, a slide detailing the process will work fine.

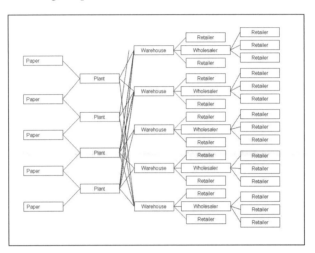

Just be sure that while you discuss the slide, you give enough time to discuss the process thoroughly. Flipping quickly through complicated slides can leave your listeners confused and frustrated.

Charts and graphs: Charts and graphs show things that are hard to describe. For example, let's say you want to show the results you've gotten for another client using a similar solution to the one you're proposing. You might show a chart or graph showing the positive results over time. You could describe your results, but the graph would allow the prospect to see those results in a more impactful way.

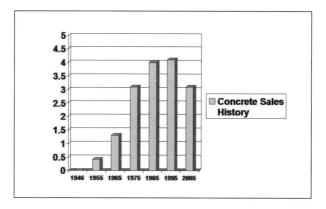

Video testimonials: If you can get a happy client to testify on your behalf on camera, do it! Sure, you can read the quote from the happy client, but the impact of seeing the president of another company talking about how great you are is quite impressive. I worked with a construction firm that built a video testimonial from the CEO of a hospital, the site of the firm's most recent job, into a sales pitch. It was impressive.

Demonstrations of your product: If you're selling something tangible, for goodness sake, bring it and let the prospect play with it. For example, if you're selling a new form of surgical glove, then bring the gloves and let the prospects play with them.

What Don't Slides Do Well?

When I was a kid, we used to go on long drives down to the beach on the Georgia coast. Occasionally, we'd pass through towns with paper mills. And boy, did those towns stink!

"How could they endure the constant stench?" I would wonder.

Of course, people do live in mill towns. They do endure the stench. How they endure it is quite simple. They get used to it. After a while, you just don't notice it any more. I suppose it's a survival mechanism.

The same is true with PowerPoint presentations. The crap we endure doesn't bother us because we're used to it. We're used to slides with dozens of bullet points. We're used to presentations with sixty slides crammed into thirty minutes. We're used to seeing spreadsheets with type to tiny too read. We've been enduring this crap for so long that it doesn't seem to bother us any more.

That doesn't change the fact that it's crap. And your prospects will be refreshed when you jettison the crap that constitutes the daily corporate presentation diet.

To my mind, a few PowerPoint archetypes constitute the crap of our corporate lives.

Avoid Bullet Point Slides: Other than the core agenda slide, I don't really put much value in bullet point slides. Sure, it helps you remember what to say, but the slides are of virtually no value to your listeners.

No one is going to remember the stuff you detail in all those bullets. You can just as easily go through the ideas without the slide. So why have the slide? I just don't get it. Guy Kawasaki, the Internet guru, investor, and former Apple executive, says that all business presentations should follow the 10/20/30 Rule. That is, your presentation should have no more than ten slides; you should speak for no more than twenty minutes, and you should never have anything smaller than thirty-point type. With no type smaller than thirty points, you can be sure you don't have too much type on any single slide.

This Is 30 Point Type!

Why are we so addicted to bullets? Everyone seems to hate them. I worked with a senior sales vice president who banned all of his sales reps from including bullet points in their presentations. "Don't murder our clients with bullets," came down the order. I asked a graphic designer why he thought corporate America is so addicted to them. "The PowerPoint software actually pushes you to create bullets," he explained. "People create their presentations by first opening up PowerPoint. They then use the visuals software to create their presentations. They then just rely on those outlines as their presentation without ever thinking of what really works visually. It's a nightmare."

Avoid Tedious Spreadsheets: This is one of those staples we just seem to accept as part of our corporate life. It's the stench that fills the mill town. I'm not saying that numbers aren't an important part of corporate America. And I'm not saying that they can't be a valuable part of a presentation, but for the most part these spreadsheets just don't do much for a presentation. They're extremely hard to read. And most of the numbers on the spreadsheet are not referenced as part of the presentation.

Date	Income	Expenses	Profit
2005-12-17	550.00	128.00	422.00
2005-12-18	222.00	124.00	98.00
2005-12-19	457.00	466.00	-9.00
2005-12-20	666.00	132.00	534.00
2005-12-21	122.00	134.00	-12.00
2005-12-22	128.00	80.00	48.00
2005-12-23	432.00	222.00	210.00
2005-12-24	256.00	121.00	135.00
	2,833.00	1,407.00	1,426.00

Avg. Profit   =AVERAGE (D2:D9)

To Create Visuals: Determine What to Say, Then Illustrate It

Creating an effective set of visuals is a two-step process. Step one, determine what you want to say and outline your message. Step two, illustrate that message in the best way possible. This may seem too obvious to even be worth saying. But the reason most slide presentations are terrible is because the presenter collapses the two steps into one.

I was working with a consulting firm to help them get ready for a presentation. "We've actually already started working on our presentation," one of the partners told me. "I'll e-mail it right over." What he sent me was a series of slides created with

PowerPoint. *In other words, in his mind, the visual aids he created were actually his presentation.*

As a result, he had created a series of visual aids that did nothing more than outline his thoughts. There was nothing particularly visual in his presentation. He didn't have a visually interesting representation of the process they were creating for their client. It was just a bunch of bullet points projected on the virtues of a piece of software. It was terrible.

So what did I do? At our first meeting, I did what I usually do in such situations. I sat down with the slides and said, "Let's go through these slides quickly just to get a sense of what this presentation is all about." Then we quickly scanned the slides, just trying to boil the presentation down to its essence. "What are the core messages?" "What specifically are you going to do to solve the client's problems?" "How are you going to show your ability to execute your plan?" "Do you have stories showing how you've succeeded in solving similar problems with other clients."

In other words, we first determine what they want to say. We then put that information into an outline based on the three-point formula outlined in the last chapter. We don't use PowerPoint to create this outline. We just use a good old-fashioned pen and a yellow legal pad. That outline usually is no longer than two legal pad pages. Sometimes I'll e-mail the outline to the client and it will be about two single-spaced pages in Microsoft Word.

Once we have the outline in place, we revisit the slides and determine which ones illustrate the key issues. Invariably, we throw out most of the slides, ending up with a far more listener-friendly pitch.

In other words, we follow an orderly process. First, we determine what we want to say. Then, we determine how to illustrate that message. When determining how to illustrate it, we should focus on one question: What can we do with visuals to help the client understand the solution?

Using Visuals with Our Three-Point Formula

Let's say that you've used our three-point formula to create your presentation. You have a nicely organized message. You're confident of what you want to say. How do you take the next step and illustrate your presentation?

Here are some basic guidelines to help guide you.

Beginning – Overview/Value Statement/ Preview

Overview

At the beginning of a pitch, you're trying to frame the business problem. Often you can frame this issue without a slide. If you're trying to win a piece of legal work and the problem is getting a good result in a bankruptcy case, you probably don't need a slide.

Let's say you're an interior design architect attempting to win a chance to transform a utilitarian office building into one that is modern and highly creative. You might start with a photograph of a boring looking hallway and then show it transformed into an exciting, creative looking hallway.

With those slides, you might say, "Our goal is to transform you from this. . . ."

"....to this."

As another example, just because you're an architect doesn't mean you automatically need to have a slide at the beginning. We worked with an architect on the interior design of a corporate headquarters building. Of course, design was a big issue in the building's construction, but the key business problem the prospect was facing was not getting a great design team.

The key business issue was building a structure over an eighteen-month period, knowing that the needs of the business might dramatically change by the time the building opens. That's a big problem. You're committing resources today for a building design when you know that the needs of the business will be different when the building is actually completed.

With that in mind, the architect had no slide to open his presentation. He simply had a well-appointed slide with the name of his firm, a "cover slide." He then said, "We've designed a lot of corporate headquarters, and when you boil it down, designing a headquarters, more than anything else, is a problem in risk management. . ." No slide is going to illustrate that point more effectively than a simple statement.

Value Statement and Preview: Bullet Point Your Three Key Messages

Remember that the value statement is a simple assertion that you're going to propose a solution to the business problem or issue detailed in the overview. This does not need a slide, as it would be nothing more than a bulleted statement saying, "We're going to detail a plan for renovating your office building and giving you great value for the money you're spending."

On the other hand, your preview is one set of bullets that you *should* put in front of your prospects. You're goal is to get your prospect to remember your three core messages. Putting the three core messages on a slide is important in helping to drill the message home. With that in mind, we recommend all presentations have a simple agenda slide. For example:

Agenda

- Your automobile leasing process is costly
- How to re-engineer your process
- How to save $500,000 a year

ILLUSTRATING YOUR THREE POINTS

To introduce each of your three points, you should return to your agenda slide, highlighting the relevant points, but then you should illustrate the points based on whether the points need to be illustrated visually.

If you're a construction firm that is trying to show the plan for getting the project done within a certain timeline, you will probably want to show your timeline for completion.

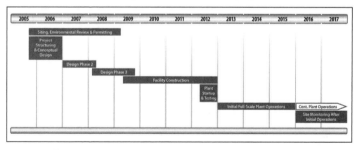

If you're proposing a new distribution system for a grocery store chain, you might want to create a flow chart that shows the current system. Then you can show a second flow chart detailing how you would change the system.

Or let's say you're trying to persuade a client to invest in a certain type of technology and you want to show a spreadsheet detailing where the investment should be. The key here is to strip the spreadsheet to its essence so it tells the story.

Here's an example: When Steve Jobs introduced the iPod, he explained why they chose to invest in a hard-drive-based player, as opposed to other options like a CD-driven player. Jobs produced a simple spreadsheet comparing the costs. His point was that for the consumer, the hard-drive-based player was actually the most cost-effective system, when looked at on a cost-per-song basis. He pointed out that the CD system costs $75, and can only hold up to fifteen songs at a time since it plays a single CD at a time. That's a cost of $5 per song. He went through the other options, ending with the hard-drive-based system, which costs $300. But he pointed out that it can hold 1,000 songs, at a cost of thirty cents a song. "That's where we think we should be," he said. This is a great example of stripping down the information on a spreadsheet to tell a story.

Player	Price	Songs	$ a Song
CD	$75	15	$5
Flash	$150	15	$10
MP3	$150	150	$1
Hard Drive	$300	1000	$.30

If you're an architect, you should show sample drawings or mock-ups of your design ideas. You should also provide photographs of similar structures or designs that you've constructed for other clients.

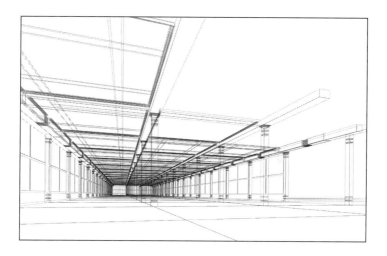

What if you're seeking to become anti-trust counsel for a large corporation? One point may emphasize that you will provide a training program to help senior executives learn how to avoid anti-trust liability. You will need to be creative to illustrate this message. When talking about avoiding anti-trust liability, perhaps you'll talk about the importance of being careful with the language in e-mails. You might include photographs of one of the famous e-mails that led to liability by Microsoft in its case.

LIMITING YOUR SLIDES TAKES GUTS AND SHOWS LEADERSHIP

I'm convinced there is an inverse relationship between the number of slides a presenter uses, and the amount of leadership and persuasion a speaker displays. I worked with an architect who had one slide detailing his design process, a flip chart where he sketched out his proposed designs, and a series of display boards showing similar buildings that he had designed. In terms of numbers of slides, it was rather sparse. But his ideas were illustrated perfectly and he displayed a clear sense of exactly what needed to be done.

More importantly, he wasn't so caught up in running through the presentation that he couldn't connect with the audience members. He was able to have a detailed conversation with the audience. He won the job because he used his thirty-minute time slot to show his leadership, display his architectural intellect, and build a relationship with the audience.

Being spare with your slides takes courage. I worked recently with a utility executive who told me that she wouldn't be caught dead going to a presentation with less than forty slides. "That's just the way our culture is around here," she said. "That's what people expect." However, that's not the way a leader thinks. And make no mistake, sales is leadership. When you're making a pitch, you're saying, "I've got an idea that will help you make money. It's simple. It's worked with other clients just like you. Here it is. Let's talk about it." Usually, a few slides are all it takes. A few slides and some guts.

How to Deliver Effectively with Slides

There's an old saying that, "A beautiful woman can turn a well-spoken man into a stammering fool." Similarly, PowerPoint can turn a bright businessperson into an inarticulate idiot. For some reason, many people simply lose their ability to communicate well when slides are on a screen.

The key to using slides effectively is to remember that they are not the show—you and your ideas are the show. The slides are just there to support you and your ideas.

With that in mind, the most important key to presenting with slides is to remember four words:

"DON'T READ YOUR SLIDES"

There are few crimes against audiences worse than simply standing in front of them and reading your slides. Your goal is to connect with the audience, but you can't do that if you're just reading your slides. When you're reading your slides, you're not looking at your audience. You're probably speaking in a droning monotone. You're not able to gauge the reaction to your ideas. You're not able to see whether anyone has a question.

It's also a colossal waste of time. You don't go to a presentation to read slides. The audience can read without you, and they can do it much faster.

If you know your presentation well, you should be able to refer to your slides and then look out at your audience.

It might go something like this:

Next, I'd like to talk about our plan for keeping your hospital safe during the construction of the new emergency room. This slide shows how we're going to keep traffic safe around your building. Look at the drawing we've done of your hospital and our traffic plan. **(As you speak, you can refer to the slide and point out how the traffic will flow. Then you will direct your attention back to the audience to discuss related issues that don't refer to the slide.)** *This is the same plan we used last year when working with another hospital in New Haven, Connecticut.*

A common mistake is to have all the information related to the New Haven Hospital detailed in bullet points. The presenter will then begin to read the bullet points, failing to connect while telling this important story.

If you're reading your slides, you're not connecting with your audience.

TELL THE IMPORTANCE OF YOUR SLIDE IN ONE SENTENCE

The way to start talking about each particular slide is to hit the listener with the key takeaway from the slide in a single sentence. State the takeaway when you first display the slide and again right before you turn to the next slide.

It will work like this. Let's say your slide is a timeline showing how you intend to finish the project in eighteen months. You display the slide. The first words out of your mouth are, "We're going to get this project done in eighteen months. That is what this slide shows." Then you go into the detail of the slide.

After discussing the slide, don't just flip to the next one. Close out the slide by restating the main point and then display the next slide. Say, "So you see, we're going to finish the project in eighteen months."

Don't Look Into the Light!

The other issue people worry about with slides is what to do when the light from the projector cuts the room in half. You've seen the problem. Your projector is on a table at the front of the room and the light from the projector is shining on the screen such that you can't walk across the front of the room without blinding yourself and briefly blocking the screen.

If you never cross in front of the light, you feel cut off from one side of the room and hence, half the audience. The solution: Try to stay to one side for about half the time and then cross over in front of the light, moving quickly to ensure that you can connect with the other half of the room.

Final Note on Slides

The most important rule of slides it that **you** are the principal visual.

No one picks a business partner based on their ability to create nice slides. With that in mind, make sure that you keep your slides simple and to a minimum. Rather than spending days creating clever slides, spend that time rehearsing.

Fundamental #3:

Show
Passion

CHAPTER 12

Passion Sells

The following story illustrates how speaking with passion separates you from your competition. Consider a scene that happens in dozens of conference rooms across America every day.

You've been sitting in a conference room all morning. You've seen three presentations so far. Every presenter has been dull. They walk in, hook up their laptops to a projector, and start narrating slides with an average level of business polish.

When the final presenter of the morning comes in, something unusual happens. He hooks up his laptop to a projector like everyone else. He has slides like everyone else.

But this presenter is different.

He seems genuinely enthused about what he's selling. He smiles when he speaks. He's speaking quickly and excitedly. He is intense. It doesn't seem like he's giving this same presentation for the hundredth time. Rather, he's delivering it in a fresh, confident, enthusiastic manner.

How are you likely to react? Chances are that you're going to sit up and take notice because this particular presenter seems so pumped. You see this presenter as distinct.

Passion distinguishes you from your competition and wins new business presentations. The fact is that most speakers don't present with much energy. They have delivered dozens of pitches in their business lives. When they stand up to give another one, it's clear that they see the pitching process as a routine part of their business lives. Another day. Another plate of spaghetti. Blah, blah, blah.

Unfortunately, corporate boredom comes through loud and clear.

To separate yourself from your competition, you must connect with your prospect by showing them how excited you are about doing work for them.

Why Passion Is Such a Separator

Passion is a separator. Qualifications usually aren't. How can this be? Many people find this criminally unfair. To understand this, consider a company that wants to build an innovative office building at a cost of no less than $75 million. They send an RFP to a number of architects and receive ten detailed proposals. From that list, they decide that three firms could do a great job. All three have impressive resumes and numerous awards for their designs. All three have clients who write glowing testimonial letters praising their incredible client service and work.

The problem, however, is that the people choosing from the three firms have no way of knowing which of the final three candidates is truly the best. They just can't tell. All three have gorgeous photographs of their projects and beautiful sketches.

The buyers can't go to *Consumer Reports* and see which architecture firm constitutes a "Best Buy."

So what do they do? How do they decide which finalist to trust with their $75 million? Since qualifications no longer matter, they pick the people they like. "We usually just choose whomever connects with us the best," a vice president for construction management told me. His job was to select architects and construction firms for a Fortune 100 manufacturer. He added, "It often comes down to style."

In talking with architects about this issue, I've seen them shake their heads in disgust at the apparent unfairness. "It's ridiculous," one fantastic designer told me. "Designing a building can't just come down to who is the best presenter. It needs to come down to who will do the best work."

Unfortunately, that attitude is common among more than just architects. Lots of businesspeople and professionals want to think that their work should speak for itself.

The problem is that buyers don't know from great work. And they certainly don't have any way of judging the quality of your work in a one-hour presentation. In fact, they're hiring you because they don't know anything about your area of expertise. Most people hiring an architect wouldn't know a great design if Frank Lloyd Wright walked them through it himself. Most business owners wouldn't know a great lawyer if Clarence Darrow himself were one of the presenters. Most people wouldn't know a great accountant if… Well, I don't know of any famous accountants. But, you get the idea.

Your prospects definitely do know with whom they connect personally. That is something they can judge quite easily. Decision-makers can easily judge which architect they like the best. They can easily judge which lawyer seems most excited about taking on their case. They can tell which contractor seems most pumped about the chance to construct their building.

As a result, personal style is a huge separator. The style trait that stands out most readily is passion. Too often, we see businesspeople delivering presentations with all the enthusiasm of a houseplant.

Freddy from Vietnam

Consider Freddy N., one of the leading accounting software sellers in the southeastern United States. A first-generation immigrant from Vietnam, this wonderful seller has a very heavy Vietnamese accent. His accent is so severe that he probably could use some remedial accent reduction coaching. I've recommended it to him.

But he has never had the coaching.

I probably wouldn't go to the coaching either if I were doing as well as Freddy. Why bother? One reason for his success is, unbelievably, that he is a very effective communicator. He is amazingly energetic in his somewhat broken English. He smiles constantly and he exudes real enthusiasm about his product.

Freddy brings that passionate attitude to every conversation. He is a high energy, fun guy to be around. During every presentation, he brings that fun guy to the pitch.

He also does a nice job of keeping his message focused. That focus, combined with his first-rate energy, makes this gentleman from Vietnam, who speaks mediocre English, very effective in sales presentations. Indeed, he is very effective when most native English speakers are not very effective at all.

Freddy and other passionate sellers understand that the products and services are often indistinguishable to their competition. That means that the key distinguishing factor isn't the product. The key distinguishing factor is the person attached to the product. From a style perspective, the key to distinguishing yourself from your competition is passion.

COMPLEX BUSINESS PRODUCTS AND SERVICES ARE NOT KITCHEN APPLIANCES

Another reason personal passion is so important has to do with what your prospect is buying. Never forget that you and your colleagues are part of the product that your customer buys.

Let's compare the process for buying complex business products and services with the process for buying kitchen appliances. When you buy a dishwasher, as a buyer, you're very interested in exactly how the product works. Why? Because you buy it, take it home, install it, and use it without anyone's help. When you buy a dishwasher, no one goes home with you to make sure that the dishwasher meets all your family needs.

On the other hand, when you buy a complex business product or service, someone comes to your office and helps you use the product. When you buy a complex software product, you're not just buying a box of CDs with a computer code that you will install yourself. You're paying for a group of *people* you don't know to come to your office and make sure that the software works and continues to work. In other words, the people attached to the product are extremely important in the decision-making process.

With professional services, the human component is even more important. If you hire an architect, you know you're going to have to spend a lot of time working with her. It's the same thing if you hire a lawyer or an accountant. When you are in the market for high-end professional services, people come with the product. You might as well make sure you like those people.

So, when purchasing a complex business product or service, you're also starting a personal relationship that will live on for months and maybe years. That's why passion matters.

To Speak with Passion, Emulate an Animated Dinner Conversation

Want to know what a passionate style is? Imagine you're having dinner with your best friend. And imagine that you're talking about something you're really excited about. Maybe it's something odd that happened at work. Or maybe you're telling about how your son just won his first tennis match and you were so excited.

As you're telling this story, chances are that you're speaking with a great deal of animation. You smile as you speak. Your eyes light up with excitement. Your voice rises up and down like a roller coaster.

That's passion. And that's the style that you need to bring to your new business pitch.

I'm the first to admit that every dinner style is different. My style is far different from yours. However, for most people, that "animated dinner conversation" style is a highly engaging, personable style.

I recently worked with a senior HR executive at a large media company who told me she is a highly conservative person by nature. "I never really get too excited," she said.

But then I asked her if she had a passion. "Shopping for shoes," she told me. "I can spend an entire day trying on shoes."

I asked her to talk to me about a great trip to the store shopping for shoes. "And I want you to pretend that I'm one of your closest girlfriends, someone who really understands your love for shoes," I added. As she spoke, I rolled the videotape.

She proceeded to speak in a highly animated, conversational, friendly style. When she saw the video, she had to admit that it was a fun, open style.

"Why can't you talk about business issues with that same passion," I asked. "After all, I know that you have a lot of passion for your work."

She paused for a long moment and then admitted she could speak that way. "But it's going to take some guts to do that," she added.

Of course, it does take courage to be good as a speaker. You have to be willing to push your limits in an attempt to connect more effectively. To set yourself apart from the competition, you have to be willing to stand out.

Find Your "Maximum You"

The animated dinner conversation style is just a way of describing the most passionate side of your personality. It might not work for everyone.

But surely there is some circumstance that draws out your intensity. Something makes you passionate, and that side of your personality is called "Maximum You." Maximum You is the person who:

- Tells your wife or husband about the ridiculous thing your boss did that day at work
- Discusses why your favorite sports team is going to have a great year
- Argues passionately for a political issue
- Cheers for your son in little league
- Gives your daughter a pep talk when she gets discouraged about something at school

When you go to a pitch, you need to bring your Maximum You.

Producing Maximum You on Cue Can be Difficult

"Easy for you to say."

Yes, it's easy for me to urge you to become "Maximum You." I also realize that it is difficult to do. But there are many legitimate barriers to achieving your Maximum You during a presentation.

First, there's the problem of knowing what you want to say.

When speaking with a good friend, you're not trying to follow a careful chain of thought like when you're delivering a pitch.

If you're arguing about which team is better, the Red Sox or the Yankees, you're not worried about carefully hitting all your points. It's bar talk. You can forget about the content and let it rip. Indeed, many of our clients tell us they can't "be themselves" unless they know their material extremely well. The moral here, of course, is that in a formal presentation setting, it's imperative to know your material extremely well, which means you must practice. Practicing like crazy is the final fundamental that separates you from your competition.

Another barrier, of course, is the stage fright that accompanies public speaking for most people. Couple stage fright with the fact that, during a new business pitch, money is at stake, and you have a situation in which nerves can be a substantial problem. Since practice is the most important way to overcome stage fright, the moral once again is to practice like crazy. We'll address rehearsal and nerves in the final section of this book.

Finally, most of the speaking we do in our daily lives is two-way. Normal daily conversation goes something like this. "What do you think of the story on the front page of the newspaper?" "I don't know. It's really disturbing. I never knew that things are getting so out of hand. What do you think?" And it goes on from there. We're used to speaking in a "back and forth" pattern.

But public speaking changes all that. Suddenly, we're expected to carry both sides of the conversation. Dialogue has become monologue. And we don't do it very well. Once again, we're taken out of our game. Being "ourselves," especially our "maximum selves" is hard.

All of these factors make it extremely difficult to be "natural" in front of an audience. After all, giving a pitch or a presentation just doesn't feel natural.

How do We Learn to Be Our "Maximum Selves" in a Speech? Acting and Practice.

That's a million-dollar question with a simple answer. We learn to act. And we practice like crazy.

Many of the techniques that help people become better public speakers are acting techniques. In fact, many great public speaking teachers were former, failed actors. Dale Carnegie, the most famous public speaking coach of all time, was a sometime actor who figured he could make more money by teaching businessmen in the early 1900s to speak by using some acting techniques he had learned. Another early and successful public speaking coach was Dorothy Sarnoff, a Broadway actress who started Speech Dynamics, in New York City. She had once starred on Broadway in *The King and I* with Yul Brenner.

In a sense, the public speaking skills coaching business has not evolved much since those early days. The most important innovation is technological. Videotaping equipment has become very simple and easy to use. As a result, it's easy to show people what they look like. But other than that, we're still using acting techniques to get people to improve the way they communicate.

Through acting techniques, you get the feel for being yourself in uncomfortable settings. We want you to learn how to "fake" being relaxed. We want you to learn how to make your face look relaxed, even if you're not. We want you to learn how to make your voice sound natural, even if you don't feel particularly natural standing in front of a room of critics. Finally, we want you to learn how to move naturally and in a relaxed manner, even if you don't feel relaxed.

All of this takes a little acting and a lot of practice.

CHAPTER 13

The Voice is the First Key to Passion

Without a doubt, the most important communication tool you have is your voice. How you sound is everything, because the energy in your voice alone can sell your ideas.

I once listened to a sales pitch my client videotaped. "When we delivered it, it didn't go over well," said the managing partner of this large consulting firm. "Can you tell us what went wrong?"

While the content of the presentation wasn't horrible, the problem was in the speakers' tones of voices. They all spoke with the enthusiasm of someone reading the telephone book. If you sound bored by your ideas, you certainly can't expect your prospect to be excited.

The importance of sounding excited is a lesson that is not lost on the owners of the television shopping networks. QVC and The Home Shopping Network are both television channels whose business model is quite simple. Get really excited about a bunch of stuff and watch people start to call in to buy it. I own a "Fry Daddy" deep fryer myself. I bought it because the guy selling it on TV was so excited about the French fries he made, that I had to own one. I think I made one batch of fries and then put it in the basement.

I'm not saying that you should sound like a television huckster. But I am saying that vocal excitement is critical to a sales pitch.

I mentioned earlier that I had once watched four construction firms pitch for a chance to build a new elementary school in Boca Raton, Florida. I mentioned that all four firms had horribly organized messages. What I didn't mention was that one of the teams did find a way to distinguish itself—with passion for the job.

One of the teams had a young project manager who talked about how excited he was to build the project. "I grew up in the neighborhood where the school is going to be located," he told the board. His passion came through in his voice. The superintendent, who was another team member, also spoke with energy and enthusiasm. Their passion made their team stand out from the rest. They won the job because of voice energy.

How to Boost Your Vocal Passion

Acting exercises are essential to learn how to boost vocal passion. These are designed to get people to speak at the "maximum you" level. Actors have been doing vocal exercises such as these for centuries.

Your Voice as a Roller Coaster

Injecting passion makes your voice resemble a roller coaster with lots of movement. That movement keeps the audience tuned in. Think about it. Have you ever fallen asleep on a roller coaster? Of course not. That's because too much is going on. You're speeding up and slowing down; curving left and then right—sometimes you're upside down. There's so much action you'll never doze off.

The same is true with your voice. If your vocal pattern is action packed, speeding up and slowing down, getting louder and soft, pausing for emphasis, your audience will not doze off.

The problem, of course, is that most business peoples' voices don't sound anything like a roller coaster. Instead, their voices are more like a freight train rumbling through Iowa. Clickety-clack. Clickety-clack. Clickety-clack. Most people speak with a boring monotone voice that puts the audience to sleep.

In our workshops, we combat monotone voices with a classic voice coaching/acting exercise. The idea is to put some action into that monotone. Participants read a simple script, which forces them to vary speed and volume.

Please read these aloud as suggested:

Read Loud
Volume adds emphasis to an important word or phrase.

Read Soft
A whisper acts as a magnet and draws the audience to you.

Read Fast
Speaking rapidly excites and energizes the audience.

Read Slow
A slow rate of speech creates a mood of awe and wonder.

Read with Pauses
A pause shows poise. . .control. . .confidence. . .use it. . .master it.

It's amazing how difficult this is for some people. For example, someone will read the first two parts of the exercise. They know they're supposed to read loudly and then get down to a whisper.

But they won't be able to do it. They will read each sentence with the exact same volume.

I'll turn to the person sitting next to the participant who just read and say, "How did she do?"

"No variation at all."

The reader will look stunned. He is completely convinced that his voice was loud and then soft.

"Did it feel like you were getting loud and soft?" I'll say.

"Yes."

Yet everyone in the class will agree that his voice didn't change at all. I've seen this happen enough times to know that the person really did believe that his voice was getting louder and softer. In his head, I'm certain his voice is changing volume. The problem is that this person, like most of us, doesn't really know how he sounds to the outside world. Most of us have listened to our own voices on a tape recorder only to recoil saying "I don't really sound like that!" But we do. We just don't have a true sense of how we really sound.

It's important to work on varying one's voice to learn to control how you sound.

Consider someone who plays trombone. I've always been amazed by trombonists because they have to learn to find the notes on a slide. They have to get a feel for how to produce a certain note. And it's only with a great deal of practice that they can learn to produce that note.

The same is true with the voice. Think of your voice as an instrument. The reason most of us have so much trouble with the "loud," "soft," "fast," "slow," and "pause" drill is that we don't have very good control over our vocal instrument.

To get better control, we urge our participants to exaggerate as they read. When they get to the "loud" part, we urge them to get extra loud. When they get to the "soft" part, we urge them to get extra soft.

Even that is difficult because participants feel they're shouting too loud, or whispering so that no one can hear. But other participants agree that the speaker's voice is much improved. Learning to control the voice is something actors call "learning the instrument."

Exercises to Learn the Instrument

Here are some additional exercises. Record these on a tape recorder, and then play it back. If you don't hear a significant change in the volume or the speed, do it again. The change in your voice should be very pronounced.

Start Fast, then Slow Down
The reason your distribution system is ineffective is . . . your centers. . . are. . . poorly. . .distributed.

Start Slow, then Speed Up
The reason. . .your. . . distribution system. . .is ineffective is. . . your centers are poorly distributed.

Start Loud, then Get Soft
FOR FIFTEEN MONTHS, YOUR SOFTWARE HAS BEEN RUNNING at a 90% efficiency rate.

Start Soft, then Get Loud
For fifteen months, your software has been running AT A 90% EFFICIENCY RATE.

Start Soft, Pause, then Get Loud
For fifteen months, your software. . .HAS BEEN RUNNING AT A 90% EFFICIENCY RATE.

Pausing and Picking out Key Words

Once you've learned how to vary speed and volume, the next step is to start playing with how to "punch" certain words with extra volume and pauses for emphasis. Once again, the goal here is to learn how not to speak in a monotone.

News anchors have long understood the need for "punching" and "pausing." Sometimes, right before the news program cuts away for a commercial, you will see the anchor at her desk writing on slips of paper. That writing isn't just for show; she is reviewing the scripts and making marks where she should emphasize certain words.

Here's a classic vocal training exercise. Read the following sentence, punching the underlined words, and pausing at the double slashes. Give the bold, underlined words an extra hard push.

For *fifteen months*, //your software // has been running at a ***90 percent*** // efficiency rate.

The purpose of these exercises is to train your voice to be more like a roller coaster and less like a slow freight train.

A More Organic Approach to Revving up the Voice

Vocal exercises are a great way to give you a feel for making your voice more exciting. But it's a mechanical approach. We don't want you writing out an entire presentation, and then underlining key words and inserting double slash marks for pauses. Once you get a feel for how to make your voice exciting, you have to learn how to do it automatically.

To learn to exude passion automatically, try another acting exercise. In our classes, we ask our clients to play a role and really ham it up, varying their voice volume and speed as well as throwing in several pauses. For example, we'll ask someone to play the role of a lawyer making a closing argument, a CEO chewing out his team after a poor quarterly performance, or a coach motivating his team at halftime.

In this case, people rev up their voices by being someone they're not. It's acting! We find that it is often easier for people to become a dramatic television lawyer like they've seen on *Law and Order,* than to just be a more dramatic version of themselves. The wonderful thing about this exercise is that people are almost always successful at role-playing *someone else* being dramatic. When they really get into the roles, they usually do the voice variety stuff (loud, soft, fast, slow, pause) without prompting. The drama brings it out for them.

Of course, the goal isn't to learn how to imitate a lawyer. The idea is the dramatic voice that you learn from imitating a lawyer begins to overflow into how you communicate about business issues.

It works. During workshops, we'll have a client do their best imitation of a lawyer conducting a closing argument. Then, midway through the exercise, we'll have them begin speaking about something related to their business. Usually, they are able to maintain that same level of dramatic intensity.

But Don't I Sound Like an Idiot?

Many people are concerned that they sound like an out of control "used car salesman" when they rev up the energy. In truth, they sound nothing like a used car salesman; there is, however, a disconnect between how they *think* they sound and how they *actually* sound.

This goes back to the idea that unpracticed speakers don't have much control over how they sound. When they are doing it right, they feel like they're going overboard. Inevitably, when we show them how they look on tape, they admit they actually look and sound quite good.

The reason it feels so strange is that they're just not used to speaking with such energy during a public speaking situation. Just as a new golf swing feels strange, great voice energy also feels odd.

Practice helps you overcome the weird feeling. Rehearse your presentations on camera so you can continually see how you're coming across. If you don't, you're going to lapse into what feels comfortable. Unfortunately, comfortable is often flat and boring.

"But I Don't Think Other People Do it That Way"

Most people can improve the quality of their voice energy. The big barrier is *willingness to do it*. I was working with a middle-level banking employee who, when she saw how she looked and sounded on tape, admitted that she came across as a much more dynamic communicator.

"But I don't think I can do that when I return to work," she said.

"Why not?"

"What will people think?" she said. "I don't know if I want to stick out that much. I'm afraid that people will think I've changed."

"Of course," I said. "You will have changed. You will have changed into someone who communicates like a leader."

Then I looked at her and said this: "I have one question for you. And only you can answer it. Are you willing to be that good?"

That scared her. She wasn't willing to be the kind of communicator who stood out from the crowd. But where she saw it as "standing out," I simply saw it as being a leader.

Another version of the same objection is the claim that, "We just don't do it that way here." I was working with a lawyer and urging her to boost her energy. It was not going well. I urged her to go to a "10" on a 10-point scale. But she wouldn't go there. Then I urged her to go to a 15. Still no luck.

I was about to give up and just laid it out for her like this. "I don't really know why you've hired me to become a better speaker when you refuse to do what it takes to become better. You clearly don't want to speak with more energy. But more energy is what you need."

She was a little stunned at how I put it, but then she said, "Look, I understand what you want me to do. But I just don't think lawyers normally speak that way."

"Actually," I said. "You're right. Most lawyers don't speak this way. But most lawyers are terrible speakers."

Indeed, most people in business are not good at this. But I'm not writing a book so you can be average. If you want to live your life on the fat part of the giant Bell curve of corporate America, stay with your current approach. You don't need me for that. I'm here to teach you how to be the kind of communicator who connects with clients and wins business.

We hear people claim that, "that kind of speaking style doesn't fly in this business" all the time. I disagree. I worked with a senior vice president for compliance for a large bank. Certainly, a major, international bank qualifies as an incredibly conservative business environment. And like many people in business, he needed to increase his vocal energy as well as facial energy. He was coming across as flat, and when he saw himself on camera, he immediately saw the problem.

"I'm boring as heck," he said. He was immediately interested in becoming more engaging. And when I urged him to ramp up the energy to a "10" he did it immediately.

The difference between the banking vice president who embraced the training and the reluctant lawyer had nothing to do with the relative conservatism of their industries. Rather, the banking vice president knew he wanted to be a business *leader*. And leadership requires standing up and being counted as a great communicator.

It's takes guts to be good at this. It takes guts to stand out. It takes guts to separate yourself from your competition.

Vocal Energy Cures Many Problems

If you give many sales presentations, chances are you will settle into a routine. Grinding it out every day is tough. And there's danger that you will lapse into a rather dull business monotone in the way that you present. It's hard to be pumped every day.

But you have to be. Voice energy is the most important element of your presentation style. Great voice energy alone can lift your presentation from dull to highly effective.

I often feel that low energy would not be so common in business if everyone approached a new business pitch the way a professional baseball player approached an "at bat." Think about the mental pressure that every Major League batter faces. Every time he steps to the plate, he knows he has to perform because there are hundreds of young, hungry players out there waiting to take his place. He doesn't have to hit it out of the park every time, but he has to bring intensity to the ballpark every day. If his performance lags for any prolonged period, he's done; his career is over.

Most people in business don't approach their jobs with anywhere near the intensity of ball players. I wonder, however, if people did consider their job to be on the line every day whether it would make a difference in the vocal energy they brought to the pitch. I suspect it would.

Voice energy is the closest thing you will find to a pitch panacea. I present two to five times a week. Often my presentations last all day. And there are many days where I don't really feel great. I'm tired. But as an entrepreneur who teaches presentation skills, I do have an acute sense that every presentation needs to be very good. I don't feel like I can afford an "off" day. And the one thing that I always remind myself of is that I can always bring lots of energy. I can always "turn it on." And it works. No matter what, my presentations always work because of that voice energy.

With that in mind, present with loads of voice energy to ensure that your pitches always come across well. Pitch as if your career were on the line.

CHAPTER 14

How to Look Passionate

Sounding passionate is important. But *looking* passionate is also important. Your excitement for the opportunity must be evident in your face, your eyes, and the rest of your body.

So let's start with the face. After the voice, facial energy is the most important tool you have for connecting with your prospects. If you speak with a flat expression on your face, you should work to change it.

Humans are incredibly attuned to facial expressions. That includes your prospects. In a study in Great Britain, scientists took routine objects and held them in front of infants faces. At the same time, the scientists measured the babies' brain waves to indicate how interesting each baby found the object. For example, they would hold a cup in front of a baby and measure the brain waves. Then they would do the same thing with a pen, a book, a fork, etc. Finally, they would put a photograph of a human face in front of the baby. The brain waves would run up off the charts.

I tell you about this study because it shows just how attuned we are to the face. Even as infants, we are fascinated with the face.

We have an enormous ability to be visually expressive with our face. Psychologist Paul Ekman has determined that there are forty-three muscles used to make facial expressions. Those muscles can create 10,000 visible facial configurations, of which 3,000 are meaningful.

Yet in business, most of us rely on only one expression, the bland "business face." Pitching with a bland expression is almost always hazardous to your pitch.

Indeed, poor facial energy isn't just hazardous to winning business, it's hazardous to keeping your job. A couple of years ago, a CEO client of mine wanted me to help one of his in-house lawyers.

"He's a great lawyer," this CEO told me. "I want to move him up to be a top business executive on our team, but he has a problem. He pisses off our customers. They think he's arrogant. I want you to fix him."

I get these kinds of requests quite often. Many people see our business as something of a "charm school." And to some extent, it is.

When I met with this lawyer, I started the session the way I always do, by asking him about his background and his work. While I'm certainly interested in understanding the person's background and building a personal relationship, I'm also interested in seeing how the person communicates.

It was immediately obvious to me why this lawyer was ticking off his company's customers. As he spoke to me, he had a completely blank, almost bored looking expression on his face. He looked like an arrogant jerk.

To help people like that, you need to show him what he looks like. I had him sit across from me and give me a briefing on a legal issue. I videotaped the conversation.

Then I showed him the tape.

The tape was rolling no more than thirty seconds when he said, "I get it." He was shaking his head. He had no idea that his bland facial energy was making him look so intimidating. And his facial energy is all that we worked on together.

Facial Energy's Impact Is Unavoidable

You need to control your facial energy because your prospects will react to it. They can't help themselves; it is an automatic reaction. In our workshops, we pair participants up, with one as the "speaker" and the other as the "listener." While the speaker talks, we have the listener watch with a completely bland expression. No smile. No reaction. Just blankness. We have the speaker talk about their favorite food. Then after fifteen seconds, we have the listeners suddenly act "fascinated," by smiling, nodding their heads, saying "Wow, that's really interesting," etc.

Try it with a friend. You'll be amazed at how negatively the bland expression affects you. And that's just during a silly little exercise. The point is that if such a silly facial exercise can have such impact during a training session, consider the impact of your facial energy when you're in a "live" situation with a prospect.

How Do You Fix Your Facial Energy?
Exaggeration

The way to improve flat facial energy is through another classic acting exercise—exaggeration. In our workshops, we have clients deliver a presentation with exaggerated facial energy. I tell them, "When you deliver the presentation this time, I want you to think about delivering the message with your face. I want to see your eyebrows pumping up and down. I want to see you squinting your eyes. I want to see every part of your face moving."

As with the exaggerated vocal energy, it will often feel strange, but it will look good. Weak communicators don't have the facial control to really convey their feelings particularly well.

In a sense, you need to learn how to exercise your "smiler" muscles. One of my own challenges was improving my facial energy. When I left law practice to get into the public speaking business, I worked with my firm's coaches to help improve my own skills. When I saw myself on camera I was stunned at how bland I looked as I spoke. In a way, I was a typical lawyer, too serious.

If my grandfather were living, he would have said, "Son, you look like you were weaned on a pickle." My face had a sour look.

In our workshops, when I tell people this story, they are usually amazed. "You seem so smiley and happy when you present," they tell me.

"That's because I worked on smiling," I tell them. I spent a month walking around smiling all the time. When I brushed my teeth in the morning, I would practice smiling. When I went through the drive-through at the fast food restaurant, I smiled at the attendant. When I bought my newspaper at the little newsstand in our building, I would smile at the lady. I smiled constantly. My cheek muscles actually ached, I smiled so much.

It became a habit. Now, smiling is a natural thing for me. People often snicker when I tell them that I practiced smiling. But that's exactly what I did.

What if You Don't Know How to Smile? Force It!

I've had people tell me that they never smile.

One client told me, "I'm just not a smiley person."

I suppose that there are people who never smile, and if you're really one of them, then you probably shouldn't be reading this book. You probably should be spending your time visiting a shrink.

Most of the time when people tell me they never smile, what they actually mean is that they are serious people and they don't see business as a time for smiling. But I catch these same people smiling all the time during business conversations.

"I wish I had my camera running right now, because you're smiling and speaking with lots of facial energy," I will say. Sometimes, I'll have a witness and they'll confirm my observation.

They're caught. The fact is that virtually everyone smiles while speaking, at least occasionally. The problem is that in public speaking situations, we all have a difficult time speaking the way we "normally" speak. We become more conservative. We become more serious. We try to live up to whatever image we have in our mind of a "serious business executive."

Your "communication game" is at its best when you're relaxed and chatting excitedly with friends. To approximate that natural style when you're delivering a presentation, you have to force that smile and facial energy. If you do it enough and practice enough, that natural style will start to feel normal when you're in "unnatural situations" like in a pitch.

Don't tell me that you never smile. As Michael Corleone said in *The Godfather II*, "It insults my intelligence."

Eye Contact That Wins Business

Passion is important. But that passion has to connect. Passion without connection is not going to help you get the job. That's where eye contact comes in.

Sometimes I feel like telling people that they should physically grab their prospects by the shirt and say, "Pay attention to my presentation. I want you to understand these ideas because they can help your business succeed. So listen!"

Of course, you can't do that, and I would never suggest such a thing. That's why eye contact is so important. The closest you can come to physically grabbing someone and saying, "Pay attention" is making strong eye contact. Indeed, great eye contact is the most intimate thing you can do during a presentation.

While most people in business do okay with eye contact, they don't maximize their connection with the client by holding eye contact long enough. Most businesspeople just look out at their audience and graze them with their eyes, never really connecting with anyone longer than a fleeting moment.

The idea is to make eye contact long enough for the person to feel as if you've connected with them, and to give you some sign that you've connected. Maybe it's a nod. Maybe it's a smile. Maybe they stick out their tongue at you. You just want to connect.

Great eye contact happens when you look at individual members of the audience long enough to feel like they are responding to you. As I write this section of this book, I'm on a flight from Chicago after delivering a program on creating and delivering new business pitches to a group of prominent architects.

In demonstrating the type of eye contact that was necessary, I looked around the room and connected with Ingrid, an interior designer from Frankfurt, Germany. As I spoke, I maintained the eye contact long enough until I saw her beginning to smile. "Now, I've got you," I said. "I'll move to someone else now."

We do an eye contact exercise in our workshops that illustrates powerfully how important and how often difficult it is to make appropriate eye contact with members of your audience. We have one of our participants stand in front of the group. Then we ask all members of the group to raise a hand.

"You should talk about what you did on your summer vacation," we tell the participant. "As you look at each person you need to make eye contact long enough to get them to put down their hand. And they won't put their hand down unless *they feel the connection.* If you just graze past their eyes without really holding it, they are going to leave up their hands. You need to hold the eye contact *through a thought.*"

It's an interesting exercise because many of the participants find it very difficult to get those hands to go down. Sure, they make eye contact, most people do, but they don't hold it long enough. Usually, they make the eye contact quickly and move to the next person, but then they realize that the person they just left still has her hand up in the air. For most people, to get the hands down, you really have to hold it longer than they are used to or comfortable with.

That's the point. What you think is comfortable in terms of eye contact is probably not enough to give your listener a sense of connection.

A good rule of thumb is to hold the eye contact **five seconds** before moving on. For those who aren't used to it, this will seem like a long time. Perhaps it will feel inappropriately long, but it won't bother your listeners. To the contrary, they'll just get the very nice sense that you're connecting with them in a personal way.

Don't Just Focus on the Key Decision-maker. Spread Eye Contact Around

When you're speaking to a panel of decision-makers, the only safe thing to do is to assume that everyone in the room will collaborate on the final decision. With that in mind, you should distribute your eye contact to everyone, trying to connect with all listeners at different times.

When I was practicing law, I sat in on a pitch from an accounting firm. The accountants had a very nice presentation on what they saw as the future of the electric utility business, an issue that was incredibly important to our client. These accountants were seeking the chance to be considered as litigation consultants.

There were ten people in the room listening to the pitch. There was one particular person who technically "controlled" the matter. Everyone worked for him, *but no one was the single decision-maker.* We all worked in collaboration. Everyone contributed in their own way, and there were three or four people who single-handedly could give a consultant the "thumbs down."

Furthermore, from the perspective of the accountants making the pitch, it would have been impossible for them to know which of the listeners would have been the key decision-makers. One of the key players was a third-year associate who had a great deal of experience in the energy business before going to law school.

So if the speakers had decided that one person was the key decision-maker and gave that person the most eye contact, they ran the risk of hacking off everyone else.

When I speak with consultants who advise clients, all of them tell me the same thing. You shouldn't underestimate the quiet person sitting in the back of the room saying nothing. That person might have the ear of the chairman.

What If Someone Won't Connect with Me? Try To Connect. Then Ignore Them!

Sometimes you're going to have people who refuse to make eye contact with you. Either they're fixated on their BlackBerry or they are reading a document. Who knows why they won't connect. Maybe they just don't feel comfortable with eye contact.

Regardless, you still need to try. And if they refuse to connect back, then just ignore them. Don't let that person distract you.

Early in my career as a public speaking coach, I was conducting a workshop with about ten participants. And while I was very high on my own skills as a presenter, there was one participant who sat in the front row with his eyes closed! Let's be clear, he wasn't just looking away or otherwise failing to make eye contact. He had his eyes completely closed as if he was napping.

And for about half an hour I found it quite distracting. I used several facilitator tricks including standing right next to him as I spoke. Nothing worked. I couldn't make him pay attention. Finally, I decided to ignore him. I didn't want to get distracted and have the program ruined for the others.

It takes two people to connect. And no matter how good a presenter you are, there are some people with whom you just won't connect.

How to Prompt Eye Contact from "Tough Customers"

Of course, you want to try to make some eye contact with everyone, even the "tough customers." There are several things you can do to prompt the listener to look at you. Once they look up, you can make the strong eye contact that can help you build the relationship.

The most important thing you can do to prompt eye contact is to have a presentation that focuses on the prospect's business needs. Most presenters fail to connect simply because their content isn't relevant to the listener. Focus your presentation solely on solving the listener's problems and your prospects most likely will be looking right at you, hanging on every word.

Another thing that will prompt eye contact is to build some interaction into the presentation. Think of some things you'd like to ask your prospect during the presentation. "Have I properly summarized the business problem?" "What do you see as the biggest business challenges?" When you ask the audience questions, they have to interact with you and make eye contact.

Finally, you need to be attuned to your audience's attention. Out of the corner of your eye, watch for that one tough customer to look up. When she does look up, look right at her, and deliver the next piece of the presentation as if it were just for her. You should have her from then on.

Gestures Can Demonstrate Passion

When people learn that I teach public speaking for a living, they often ask me, "What should I do with my hands?" My gut reaction is to say, "Who really cares? The real question is what are you doing with your voice and your face?"

Nevertheless, many people (my clients included) do worry about what to do with their hands. And I have to admit that your gestures can make you look bad if not handled correctly. Further, strong gestures can give you an energetic, passionate presence. There are several rules that will give you a strong energetic presence.

First Rule of Gestures: Don't Distract

First, let's talk about distractions. If you agree that the face and the voice are the main event, then the important thing to remember is that your hands shouldn't be pulling the audience's attention away from that main event.

My favorite story about distracting gestures comes from my days as an attorney. One day, Steve Forbes, the magazine publisher, came to our office to raise money for his presidential run. He stood as he spoke about his positions on various issues. I don't remember much of what he talked about, but I do very much remember his hands. He held them out in front of him, cupped together as if he had just captured a firefly and was trying to keep it from escaping. And every time he made a key point, he would open his hands, like he was releasing one of the fireflies.

So Forbes might say something like, "Let me tell you about my ideas on how to lower taxes." And as he would say the word "taxes" he would release a firefly and then close his hands again, and then he would do it again. And again. Releasing fireflies every time he made a point.

It was incredibly strange and distracting.

And that's the problem with bad gestures. More than anything else, they distract. And that's not good.

Gestures That Distract

Many gestures can be distracting.

- **Apple picking:** where you stab out at the air and bring your hands back quickly as though you're picking apples and putting them in a basket.
- **Velcro-elbows:** where your elbows are attached to the hips, making your hands swing around like silly looking windmills.
- **Spider fingers:** where your hands are very tight and spidery.
- **The Jimmy-leg:** where your leg is pushing forward in an awkward stance.
- **Puppy dog arms:** where your arms are at your sides and your wrists are hanging down like a puppy dog begging for food.
- **Jazz fingers:** where your fingers are spread out and palms are forward.
- **Window-washers:** where your hands move around as if you're trying to clean the windshield on a car.
- **Vanna-arms:** where you're reaching out like Vanna White turning letters on *Wheel of Fortune*.

All of these gestures can distract, and if your audience is looking at your hands, they're probably not listening to your message. That's not good.

Gestures That Make You Look Confident: Start with the Stance

Good gestures start with a good "neutral stance." A good stance is perfectly square with your feet about shoulder-width apart. Your hands should be hanging down at your sides like a bunch of bananas. Your weight should be evenly distributed between your feet. If anything, you should be "feeling" your weight on the balls of your feet. Don't lean your body forward, but just have a general forward "feel" to your body.

Neutral Stance is confident and open.

The idea with the neutral stance is to be open to the audience. This basic stance is a blank slate. Nothing distracts from your message. You are open. You are confident.

Of course, there are also many ways you should not stand.

The Schoolmarm Stance. This is a prim stance with your hands clasped in front of you like a scolding schoolmarm. It looks closed. You will find some disagreement among public speaking skills coaches on the "schoolmarm stance." Some coaches will tell you that having your hands clasped in front of you is a fine way to make *yourself comfortable.* Of course, I'm not as concerned with your comfort as how confident and open you look to the audience. The only reason the neutral stance is uncomfortable to most people is that it's new. If you look at yourself in a mirror or on tape, chances are that you'll agree that you look more confident with you hands at your sides.

The Firing Squad Stance. Some call this the "military" stance. With your hands clasped behind your back, you look defensive. It looks like you're bracing for a blow or that you're trying to shore up your courage. I met a French public speaking skills coach who saw us demonstrating this same position and told us that in France they call it "le fusillade" which means "execution." Translation? Bad body language is universal.

Fig Leaf Stance. Does this really need an explanation? Suffice it to say that it's rather defensive.

Pretzel Stance (also known as the Female Fig Leaf). This is a closed position. Once again, the goal of your pitch is to present to your prospect a sense of openness. When your arms are folded across your chest, you're closed.

Gunslinger: This is where your weight shifts toward one hip. While this position is open, it's also a little distracting. People who adopt the gunslinger position tend to shift back and forth.

Girlie Legs: This is where one leg is coyly placed in front of the other. You don't have to be a girl to do this one, but it is a very weak look. Nothing is wrong with being feminine, but we don't want to look weak. "Girlie legs" is a closed, shy, highly unconfident look.

Macho Man: This is where your hands are on your hips. This is both defensive and aggressive. Remember that the goal isn't to make you look like a stud; it is to connect with the audience. With that in mind, relax those arms and let them hang at your sides.

The Professor: This is with the hand stroking your chin in thought, another closed stance. We've also noticed that "Professors" tend to make poor eye contact. The thing is bad all around. Closed. Not connected. It's also a little pretentious. Don't do it.

What Do Good Gestures Look Like?
Big and Steady

The first word in gestures is "big." We want you to make big gestures because it makes you look confident and like a leader. There's a lot of evidence that size impresses audiences.

In fact, several studies show how height correlates to pay. One study from the University of Florida found that a person who is six feet tall on average makes $5,000 a year more than a person who is five feet five inches tall.

What I take from all of this is that size, for whatever reason, translates into "leadership presence." People tend to look at tall people as leaders.

The evidence doesn't just end there. There's evidence that respect for size is part of the natural order. There's a book titled *Worst Case Scenario Handbook* in which the authors detail how to survive various horrifying scenarios, such as when you're caught in a gun fight or if you ever need to jump off a moving train. One of my favorites is what to do if you're in the woods and you come across a mountain lion.

You should not run because the mountain lion is definitely faster than you are. What the book says to do is to reach out and make yourself look as big as possible. There is something about size that commands respect from the mountain lion.

We think that size commands respect from audiences as well. Of course, we can't make you taller. And we don't recommend getting "elevator" shoes if you're short.

But, big gestures can make you look bigger and give you the stature of someone larger.

GESTURES STEP ONE: REACH OUT

The first step to making yourself look bigger is to reach out with your gestures. Extending those arms will take up more space and make you look bigger.

Too often, we see people making tiny gestures cramped around their body. That actually makes them look smaller. And when you couple small gestures with a small person, the presenter can look extremely small and unconfident.

On the other hand, large gestures from a small person look extremely confident. I worked with a rather short president of a large health care business. He made himself look bigger than he was by carrying himself with a very erect posture and making large gestures as he spoke. Despite his diminutive size, his carriage and gestures allowed him to project a much larger presence.

GESTURES STEP TWO: HOLD THE GESTURE

The next step to making your gestures more confident is to hold the gestures longer. You don't want to flap at the air with your arms reaching and quickly pulling back. That can be extremely distracting. And, as already noted, the most important rule about gesturing is not to distract.

Reaching out makes you look big

On the other hand, when you hold the gesture, you look calm
and confident. We say that you should hold the gesture "through
the thought." Think of an umpire. How would people feel about
them if when a person slid into home, the umpire would shout
"Safe!" and then made a wimpy gesture that reached out and
dropped quickly. It wouldn't have the same effect. Similarly, we
want you to reach out and hold those gestures confidently.

Reach out and hold your gestures

GESTURES STEP THREE: REACH FORWARD

Finally, good gestures are generally forward or at least to the side, but never backward. The idea here is that you want everything to be moving forward in the direction of your listeners. Remember that the goal is "connection." With the audience in front of you, your gestures will connect more if they are in that forward direction.

The Hand Bone is Connected to the Voice Bone

As you can tell, I'm not that into gestures. I think they're the focus of too much attention. People put a lot of effort into getting their gestures right but they don't actually become substantially better presenters. On the other hand, if those same people were to put that effort into improving either their facial or vocal energy, they'd see a substantial pay-off in terms of overall effectiveness as a presenter.

And the interesting thing is that if your voice or face improves, chances are your gestures will too. We see it all the time in our workshops. Sometimes we find someone who has problems with gestures as well as vocal and facial energy. Where do we start? We certainly can't help them improve in all areas at once. We usually focus on voice energy or facial energy. We'll say, "Forget about your gestures for now. On this exercise, we just want you to focus on being as facially expressive as possible. Over-exaggerate your facial energy."

And when they do the exercise, we find that people's facial energy improves and so do the gestures!

Why? Well, it seems obvious when you've done this type of coaching for a while. Most presentation skills coaches teach the elements of presentation style separately. First, we teach vocal energy. Then we teach facial energy. Then we teach gestures and movement. This method assumes these elements stand individually and can improve separately without referencing the others. And they can.

But we also know that all of these elements are connected. How you are with your face affects how you move your hands. How energized you get with your voice impacts what you do with the hands. It's all connected! The face bone is connected to the hand bone!

That's not to say we would never tell you to improve your gestures. Sometimes people's gestures are so atrocious that something must be done. But most of the time your efforts are better spent in the true "communication zone" of your face and voice, and if you get that right, there's a good chance that your gestures will improve naturally.

And Vice Versa

The one time that I pay a lot of attention to gestures is when I'm trying to help a person energize their voice and face. Sometimes energetic gestures lead to great voice energy.

I once helped an economist who worked for a large bank. He told me he wanted to be "more dynamic when speaking of economic issues." Of course, we worked very hard to help him make the content of his presentations more interesting by using stories and analogies.

However, we also suggested that he consider getting far more enthusiastic and physical with his gestures.

"Work up a sweat," I told him.

As he spoke, he really got into it with his gestures. He moved his hands quickly and energetically, reached out, held his gestures, and just acted excited in general.

It worked! His overall vocal and facial energy improved substantially. He became a highly animated "dynamic economist."

Movement: Great Speakers Move with Purpose, and Then Stop

Like gestures, how you move isn't going to win you any business. However, it can make you look more confident and more "leader-like." That's nice, but if you're not careful, you can certainly move in a way that is annoying to your prospective client. And that's not so nice. Of course, strong movement can also give you an energetic and, yes, passionate presence.

From a coaching perspective, one major difference between gestures and movement is that it's easy to improve your movement. Unlike gestures, which people have been using incorrectly their entire lives, most people don't move much at all during their presentations. So there are few bad habits to break.

Here's the advice for movement.

Move!

That's it. Walk around as you speak. If you have a lot of space, use it. Walk to one side of the room and talk. Then when you have made a point, move to the other side of the room.

Moving does several good things for you. First, it usually helps you relax. The nervous energy dissipates somewhat as you move around. Second, it's more interesting for the listener. If you're moving, chances are that your listeners are following you with their eyes. And that's a good thing.

My infant niece, Samantha, is fascinated by the rotating fan in our house. She will stare at it for hours, smiling and googling, her legs flapping away happily. Why? Because she finds the movement interesting. The same is true for your listeners. There is something inherently satisfying about watching a moving object versus a static object.

Of course, you do have to be careful about a couple of things when you move. You want to move randomly, not pace back and forth. I had a law professor who paced back and forth along the same ten foot stretch of the lecture hall. He did it continuously through every fifty-minute lecture, four days a week for the entire semester. Out of curiosity, I checked the path he walked. He literally had worn a track in the lecture hall's carpet. You also should make sure that you do not walk in a circle, doing a box step.

The best movement pattern is to move purposefully to a spot and then plant your feet and stay there for a while. Make a few points. Then move to another spot. When we coach our clients to move more effectively, we place two or three napkins on the floor. "These are your marks," we say. "Start speaking and I'm going to give you a little direction. If I point at that napkin, I want you to walk over and step on the napkin and then plant your feet. Think of your feet being in cement. Then when I point again, you move to the next napkin."

By moving to a point and stopping to deliver a message, you avoid the annoying trap of wandering.

Presence That Sells When You're Seated

Seated presence is just like standing presence. Only you're sitting. The idea is still to be open and connected with the listener. That means sitting up and forward with relaxed open hands.

The television news anchors are fanatics about sitting up and forward. When I was promoting my first book *Even A Geek Can Speak* I went on CNN. I was in an Atlanta studio, while the news anchor interviewing me was in New York. It was my first time on a news program and one of the most interesting things was the chair they put me in. It was shaped to fit my rear end, and was tilted up and forward slightly. There was no back to the chair. It was kind of like one of those ergonomically correct "kneeling" or "posture" chairs that force you to sit forward.

I point this out because news anchors are extremely conscious of their image on television. They've thought a lot about how to come across as connected to their listeners as possible. And they've designed their furniture to force them to sit up and forward, leaning into their listeners. Next time you watch CNN or your favorite news program, notice how the anchors are sitting. They're rarely leaning back. Even if they're on a couch, they're sitting up and forward.

And while you're at it, check out their hands. They're usually spread out slightly as opposed to clasped together. Once again, the driving principle is openness and connection with the audience. Open hands are, well, more open.

Seated presence should be open and forward

"Should I 'Mirror' My Prospect?"
Sometimes—But Be Careful

Many people have heard of the concept of "mirroring." Mirroring is the idea that you can create a sense of empathy by "mirroring" your listener's movements and posture. If your prospect leans back, then you should do the same. If your prospect looks intense and leans forward, you should do the same.

Mirroring is fine. But remember that in a pitch, the idea is to sell an idea through connection and energy. If you're leaning back, it's hard to be particularly connected and energetic.

I also think that you should be wary of allowing someone else to dictate the impression you make. Remember that your job is to connect. If you walk into a room and you see a prospect who seems detached and is leaning back in his chair, you should not mirror that same type of body posture. I don't care how detached your prospect seems. You don't ever want to seem detached.

On the other hand, you should certainly be aware of the prospect's apparent frame of mind and be careful not to come across as overly intense. Your intensity could likely clash with the prospect's mood.

In the end, as always, you need to use your best judgment. Everything in this book is based on principles that should drive how you think about selling your ideas. But we're not prescribing laws that can't be broken. We're not communication Nazis.

Steps for Self-Diagnosing and Improving Style Issues

The best way to start to improve your style is to get some coaching. It's amazing how a good coach and a video camera can help a person improve in a short period.

But you don't necessarily need a coach.

A camera alone will often do the trick. As I often tell my clients, "The camera is a far better coach than I am." I'll videotape my client and let them tell me what they think before I've weighed in at all. Most of the time, they figure out exactly what I was going to say.

Here's how you can improve your style without the help of a coach.

Step 1. Deliver a part of your presentation on camera and watch it. Ideally, you should take part of a pitch you plan to give to a client. But any presentation will do.

Step 2. Look first for eye contact. If your eye contact is down at the floor or directed solely at your notes, then you have a problem that must be corrected immediately. Failure to make eye contact makes connection with the listeners impossible. Set up chairs around the room and practice making eye contact with imaginary audience members. At our offices, we have Halloween masks mounted on sticks that we place in chairs to pose as the listeners.

Step 3. Look for vocal energy. Most businesspeople have good eye contact. At least they're looking at the audience. Most businesspeople have poor vocal energy. This is where most people can make the biggest improvement. You have to sound excited about your ideas. One of the most common things that clients will say when I show them their videotapes is simply, "I don't sound very enthusiastic." To improve passion, try speaking about something you're passionate about, forcing yourself to get overly excited. Then deliver your pitch with the same level of energy. Chances are your pitch will come across very well.

Step 4. Look for facial energy. While watching a videotape of yourself, turn off the volume. Do you look excited? Or do you look bored? To fix facial energy, exaggerate. Do more with your eyebrows and your eyes. It may feel weird, but it will look great. As Billy Crystal once said, "It is better to look good than to feel good."

Step 5. Look at your gestures and movement. If everything else is great, then I doubt you'll need this step. No one with great facial and vocal energy has a problem connecting, regardless of how they move.

Final Thoughts on Style

Whether we like it or not, how we look and sound matters a lot. A researcher named Albert Mehrabian studied how humans communicate and found that 93% of the impression we make when is based on how we look and sound. Only 7% of the impression is based on the content of what we say.

Now I certainly don't think that content is unimportant. So I can't completely agree with his study. But I do think that how we look and sound is critical. Over and over again, I've seen major pieces of business go to the team that comes across as the most passionate.

But the fact is that huge decisions often turn on superficial things. I once heard of an accounting firm that lost a piece of business because, as the partner told me, "Our experts didn't have enough gray hair."

The fact is that decision-makers often can't really tell who is going to do the best job. They have no idea which is the best law firm or who is the best consultant. Everyone's marketing packages are professional. Everyone has incredible references. All the contestants have incredible websites and resumes.

And now they have to make a decision as to who is better based on an hour-long presentation. With that problem in front of them, they often end up falling back on something they can judge without any doubt. While they may not judge who can pour concrete most efficiently, they certainly can judge who they like the best. And so they make a decision based on a presenter's personal style. The best presenters do everything they can to present in a style that connects.

Fundamental #4:

Involve Your Audience in the Presentation

CHAPTER 15

Making Your Presentation Interactive

There is an easy way to tell if your presentation has flopped, utterly failing to distinguish your team from the competition.

Let's say that you're almost finished with your presentation. As you're winding down, you notice that your prospect hasn't interrupted you once. Then, one of the people on the decision-making panel says, "Thanks, nice job. We really appreciate you coming. We'll give you a call when we make a decision."

And that's it.

If the last thing you hear from your prospect is some variation on a limp "we'll call you," then you've probably lost.

The best presentations always involve lots of interaction. The very best ones lose the feeling of a pitch entirely. The best presentations take on the feel of a collaborative work session in which both sides have rolled up their sleeves and are working on solving the business problem at hand.

That interactivity helps distinguish you from the competition by allowing the prospect to get a feel for who you and your colleagues are as individuals. They get to hear how you respond to questions and challenges. They see how you work and react when someone tells you that they don't like or understand your ideas. All of that interaction serves to show you as a unique property. It differentiates you.

With that in mind, one of the fundamentals of a great pitch is to make the pitch as interactive as possible. Great pitches give the prospect as much chance as possible to ask questions and interact. If the prospect doesn't seem inclined to ask questions, good presenters find ways to involve the prospect in the presentation, drawing out any objections and finding ways to build the relationship.

Interaction Is a Gauge of Prospect Interest

Why is interactivity important? It's important because no one makes a major buying decision without a great deal of interaction.

Consider the following scenario. Let's say you're hiring a contractor to do some major work on your house. You're going to renovate the kitchen, add a new bedroom and bathroom, and tear down your old deck and put up a new one. Overall, you're going to spend more than $100,000. It's a big decision, so you bring in a number of contractors to bid on the work.

Can you imagine making the decision about which contractor to hire without discussing the project with him or her extensively?

Of course not. No one makes big decisions without discussing the work in depth with the proposed vendor. That's why, as a seller, you want your prospects to interrupt you and ask questions. It's a sign that the prospect is interested in working with you and discussing the project with you. It is a sign that the buying process is proceeding properly. It also allows you to get a feel for where they are in their mental process of considering you.

One of my favorite stories about the importance of interactivity in making a sale involves the oral argument delivered by Thurgood Marshall in *Brown v. Board of Education.* This case ended up desegregating the public school system. Before becoming a Supreme Court Justice, Marshall was a brilliant and legendary advocate for the NAACP. When he stood before the U.S. Supreme Court to argue what was perhaps the most famous and important civil rights case ever, he was well-prepared with a thorough presentation.

But he never got to use it. As soon as the light went on for him to start his argument, the judges began peppering him with lots of questions, challenging his assumptions and arguments. The questioning was so intense that some might have thought that the judges were seeking a way to reject Mr. Marshall's arguments.

But just the opposite proved to be true. They were highly interested in his argument and they wanted to see whether it stood up to challenge.

The Supreme Court then sided with Mr. Marshall and the NAACP in a historic 9-0 vote. The huge number of questions was an indication of the interest in the justice's positive interest.

This concept doesn't just apply to the U.S. Supreme Court. Whenever my clients deliver new business pitches, I call and ask how they did. The first question I ask is, "Did you get a lot of questions?" If the answer is yes, then I know the presentation went well. In fact, sometimes my clients will tell me, "We really didn't even get through our presentation. They were asking questions almost the entire time." That's another indicator that the presentation went well.

Interactivity Allows You to Display Your Unique Intellect

Interactivity is not just valuable for gauging your listeners' interest in your ideas. It is also valuable because it shows your prospect something that no canned pitch can show: your intellect in action.

Consider for a moment the problem that your prospect faces in making a big buying decision:

- If you're an attorney, they're not hiring your firm's resume; they're hiring the intangible ability to solve a complex problem.
- If you're an accountant, they're not hiring your client list; they're hiring your ability to make good financial judgments.
- If you're a contractor, they're not hiring your photographs of all the successful buildings you've built; they're hiring your ability to manage a complex project to a successful and safe completion.
- If you're a software vendor, they're not buying a box of software; they're hiring your ability to help them use the software to solve business problems.

In fact, with virtually any complex product or service, your prospect is hiring your judgment and ability to solve problems. In other words, they're hiring your mind. The question is, how do they look at your mind?

They ask questions. They test your assumptions. They throw out ideas and see how you react. They find ways to "kick the tires." When a prospect hits you with a question, it's their chance to see your intellect in action.

If you wanted to hire a law firm to help you with an antitrust case, many firms could give a presentation on past successes with such cases. But those presentations usually have a canned, "old news" quality. You would think, "Sure, you won that case last year, and that shows that you have basic qualifications, just like everyone else we invited to this beauty contest, but that case had a far different set of circumstances. My case isn't exactly like that. I'm curious as to how you're going to be able to handle our circumstances. I also want a sense of what it will be like to work with you."

To give them that sense, you need to allow the prospect a chance to ask questions. He might ask, "What would you do with the fact that we have no process for monitoring our own e-mails? And what does that mean for this case?"

All of a sudden, the presentation has taken on a very different feel to the prospect. Instead of feeling canned, it feels alive. All of a sudden, you're talking about their specific business problem and giving them a sense of what they're hiring. All of a sudden, we're playing with live ammunition.

If you handle that question well, then your prospect starts to get a sense of how his case will be handled. He also gets to see your mind in action. He gets to see you thinking and responding in what appears to be an unrehearsed way.

All of a sudden, he has a way of making a real distinction between the other firms. Why? Because your competitors will respond differently to the same questions. And it's going to be obvious.

Some of the firms are going to fumble the questions completely. Some will come up with good answers, but only after the members of the team look at each other, unsure as to "who is supposed to take that one." Some will give answers that ramble and eventually land on something persuasive.

Maybe one firm will take that question and handle it quickly and simply, conveying a sense of total confidence in how to deal with that unique issue. That final firm is going to separate itself.

You need to allow people to ask questions because it allows your prospect to do something I call "tasting the wine." When you buy a bottle of wine at the grocery store, you can't taste the wine beforehand to make sure that you like it. So you pick based on the label and the price.

When making a decision in a beauty contest, companies have the same problem. It's hard to get a "taste of the wine." That means it is hard to get a true sense of a vendor's intellect before they buy. But allowing the prospect to ask questions gives a little taste, and it allows the prospect to see the vendor react and think in real time in much the same way they will have to act if they're hired. With that in mind, great presenters find ways to manufacture such authentic moments during their presentations.

Interactive Presentations are More Fun

Don't underestimate the importance of making sure your prospect enjoys the time spent with you. They know they're going to have to spend a lot of time with whomever they hire. They want to like that person.

And interactive presentations are just more fun and will tend to make your audience like you more.

The vice president of development for a large religious seminary, a university with a gorgeous campus, told me about the architectural firms that came to pitch their ideas for a new building.

"They came with a model of the campus that we could play with during the presentation," he told me. "And so we spent a lot of time moving the buildings around and imagining how the campus would look with the new building and where it should be located. It was kind of neat."

Hearing him speak, it was clear that the model was not only helpful, it was also fun.

If you were to ask people their favorite things to do, few would say, "I love listening to business presentations." So anything you can do to make the process enjoyable is appreciated. Interactivity will ensure that your listeners are engaged and having fun.

ENSURE THAT YOU GET AS MANY QUESTIONS AS POSSIBLE BY PLANNING FOR Q&A

The most important key to getting lots of interaction is to leave plenty of time for Q&A. If you have one hour with your prospect, make sure that your prepared pitch is no longer than thirty minutes. You want to be interacting with your prospect half of the time you're with them. You want to leave room for the spontaneous stuff.

At the beginning of the presentation, make sure the prospect knows that you have planned for them to ask questions. "This is an interactive presentation. I have left plenty of time for questions. So please interrupt me at any time."

Great presentations have lots of Q&A time. Remember Guy Kawasaki's presentation advice, and follow the "10/20/30 rule." Have no more than ten slides. Speak for no more than twenty minutes. And never use less than thirty-point type in your slides.

While I like the rule in general, I'm especially interested in the idea of preparing no more than twenty minutes worth of material. If he gives them an hour, what is he going to do with the rest of the time? Ask questions and discuss the ideas! The point is that the discussion is something that is expected. He won't make a major decision, such as investing in a business, without a detailed discussion.

TOO MUCH "PRESENTATION" SQUELCHES QUESTIONS

If your presentation has too much prepared information, you squelch questions. Your listeners can tell when you have too much information to deliver during the prepared time. They know when you're madly rushing through the fifty slides that you want to hit during the forty-five minutes of your presentation. They can sense your rush to finish. And so they oblige you by keeping their mouths shut.

They let you finish your presentation. They smile and thank you for coming. Then they send your on your way and never see you again. Why? They weren't able to get to know you because they didn't get a chance to ask questions or interact with you.

Encourage Your Audience to Ask Questions at Every Turn

The more responsive you are to listener questions and interruptions, the more interruptions you will get. This is a good thing. On the other hand, the more you squelch questions, the fewer you will get. That's a bad thing. You can, however, *train your listeners* to give you the level of interaction you want.

You read that right. You need to **train your prospect** to ask questions during your pitch.

To understand how to train your audience, let me first explain how comics keep an audience in stitches. Great comics don't just have great jokes, they train their audiences to laugh.

I learned this when taking a class in stand-up comedy from an Atlanta comedian named Jeff Justice. During the class, Jeff told a story about a female comic who had good material but was getting few laughs. When he heard her delivery, however, he understood the problem. She wasn't waiting long enough for the laugh. She'd give a funny line and then go right into the next one without waiting for people to stop laughing. As soon as she started up with her next line, the audience would quickly get quiet because they didn't want to miss the next joke. As she kept cutting off the laughs with her next line, she actually trained her audience not to laugh.

So what did Jeff recommend? "You have to wait for the laugh," Jeff told her. And that's what she did. Once she told a joke, she carefully waited for the laughter to die down. As a result, her laughs got longer and longer. Her material wasn't any different; she was telling the same jokes. But after working with Jeff, she learned that telling great jokes isn't enough. You also have to create an environment in which the audience can laugh.

Similarly, you can create an environment in which your prospects will ask more questions. You do that by eliminating behavior that squelches questions.

Indeed, just as you can squelch laughter, you can also squelch questions. Many sellers sabotage their presentations by sending explicit, implied messages that questions are not welcome.

I've already noted that it's important to leave plenty of time for Q&A. Indeed, one of the most common ways to squelch questions is simply to create a presentation that is too long. I've even seen presenters begin their pitch by saying something like, "Well, we only have an hour and I have a lot of slides, so let's get started." Statements like that send a very clear message that you really don't want questions.

Another way to squelch questions is to openly avoid them. I've seen presenters blatantly avoid taking questions, waving them off, ignoring them, or even saying "Please hold the questions until the end." If a prospect said that to me, here's how I would respond. "No problem. I think we can end this right now. This meeting is over. You lose." Remember, the pitch is not for the presenter's benefit. It's for the prospect's benefit.

One of the most ridiculous presentation inventions is the "parking lot." "I'm going to put that question in the parking lot until later." Indeed, I've even seen professionally manufactured "parking lots" that you can buy for your presentations. These are whiteboards with lines drawn to look like a parking lot. When you get a question for the parking lot, you're supposed to write it down in one of the "parking spaces."

Theoretically, you're supposed to return to the parking lot at the end of the presentation and answer the questions. Of course, the problem with the parking lot is that the prospect doesn't want to see his question go into the parking lot. He wants his question answered. He's obviously having a problem understanding something and needs your help before the presentation continues.

Similarly, questions go stale in the parking lot. You return to the questions at the end of the presentation and it's often unclear what the context was around the question.

The final problem with the parking lot is that you often don't have the time to get back to the questions. In fact, the entire concept behind the parking lot is to move the presentation along because "we've got to get through this" in the time we have. You end up running out of time.

My apologies to anyone reading this who loves the "parking lot." I run into you guys periodically. But it's time to move on. It's a rotten idea. Always has been.

If You Get a Question, Drop Everything and Answer It!!!!!

The parking lot is the antithesis of one of the most important concepts in pitching: *questions from the prospect are gold*. If you saw gold on a sidewalk, would you walk by it thinking, "I'll get to it later?" No! You would pick it up.

Similarly, when you get a question from your prospect you should do two things. First, you should thank God, the Force, or whatever higher power you're into (if you're an atheist, then just thank your good luck), that your prospect has asked something. It means that they're really interested. Second, you should answer the question.

That's right. A question interrupting your presentation is a golden gift that should not be squandered. That question means that the prospect is interested in your presentation. It most likely means the prospect is thinking something like, "Hmmm. This presentation is interesting and is piquing my interest. I'm seriously considering the proposal they're laying out. But there is something I don't understand. I can't go forward hearing this if I don't get something cleared up. I'm going to raise my hand now and interrupt to clear this up before we go any further." When you realize that this is the subtext, how can you not want to stop and answer the question?

Or think of it this way. Your presentation is like a train ride through the Wild West carrying your prospect to the magical city of "Everybody Gets Rich, California." And the prospect is on the train, riding along happily, hoping to arrive at that happy destination where you will solve all of his problems.

But wait!!! Some mean looking bandits have just boarded the train in the form of a MISUNDERSTANDING! Oh no! Everything is at risk! The nasty MISUNDERSTANDING Bandits have made your prospect consider jumping off the train if the Bandits can't be eliminated. So you've got to get rid of those nasty MISUNDERSTANDING Bandits by answering the question and clearing up the misunderstanding.

And you need to do it now! You can't wait! You can't say, "Don't worry about those MISUNDERSTANDING Bandits! We'll deal with them later! We'll ask them to sit quietly in this special "parking car" and we'll deal with them later." No, the MISUNDERSTANDING Bandits are disturbing the prospect now! Sequestering the Bandits won't help. Your prospects are thinking of getting off the train. So you have to eliminate the Bandits by answering the question right now.

At least, that is what you should assume the prospect is thinking. And with that in mind, your job is now to clarify any misunderstandings by answering the question and thereby clearing away any barrier to moving forward in the prospect's mind. If you can successfully clear away that barrier, then you're that much closer to closing the deal.

Answering Questions Immediately Encourages More Questions

Like many dogs, my dog Rocko is fairly easily trained. All you have to do to get him to learn a behavior is give him an enthusiastic scratch behind the ears. He loves approval from his master. Whenever he sits on cue, I give him a scratch behind the ears and he loves it. When he heels correctly, I praise him with a scratch behind the ears and an enthusiastic "good dog." When he lies down properly, once again, I just praise him.

Humans are the same. Positive reinforcement encourages behaviors that you like. If you want people to ask questions, you need to give them a figurative "scratch behind the ears." And the most important positive reinforcement for getting more questions is simply answering all questions enthusiastically. An enthusiastic answer is a reward that will beget further questions and that's what you're hoping for.

That doesn't mean you need to say "Great question!" Indeed, we would prefer you didn't say "Great question" because it can sound patronizing and insincere, especially if you're saying it constantly. Instead, just act as though the questions are great. Take every question seriously, and ask whether you've answered clearly. Just as important, wait for follow-ups to the questions and answers.

BUT WON'T I RISK LOSING CONTROL OF THE PRESENTATION?

Many presenters worry that they might lose control of their presentation if they allow too many questions. My first response to this concern is this: "What do you mean by losing control?"

If "losing control" means handling lots of questions from your prospect, then by all means lose control. Get way out of control. Get wildly, crazily out of control.

Remember, the presentation is for your prospect's benefit. If they have many questions, why would you not want them? You know your presentation is going well if your prospect is asking many relevant questions.

BUT THAT'S NOT WHAT I MEAN!

Of course, I understand that many people worry about losing control in the sense that they worry about the presentation truly going "off the rails." They worry that the questions will get so arcane and irrelevant that the presentation will be a waste of time for everyone. *"How did we get into a situation where we were discussing the colors of the brick we chose on our last construction job?"*

Certainly, it is a risk that having lots of interaction in a presentation can lead to the presentation "going off the rails."

But that risk can be managed in several ways.

The first way to manage the risk is to use a technique we call "bridging." If things get too out of hand, you bring the conversation back to "reality" by simply "bridging" back to a key point. By this, we mean you can simply say, "Well, we're making good points here, which brings me back to the second core thing that we're going to do to help you achieve your goals."

Note that it doesn't really matter if, in fact, the conversation really was naturally "bringing you back to the second core thing." Who cares? Your listener isn't parsing your sentences so carefully as to notice whether the segue is natural or logical. If the presentation has truly gone way off track, most likely your listeners will appreciate that you are taking control. No one will give it a second thought.

The next way that you manage the risk of losing control is simply to ensure that you're preparing a presentation of the proper length. If you're preparing a presentation that will only last half of your allotted time, then you will have plenty of time to answer all questions and still get through your presentation. Presenters who fear losing control are usually the ones who need a lot of control in order to get through all the information they're trying to cram into the short bit of time they have with the prospect. Leaving plenty of time for questions is also a way of leaving plenty of time for your listener to ask questions and, if necessary, get off track.

Finally, you can manage the risk of an interactive presentation by being very prepared for the questions that you will receive. One reason people fear interaction is that they're not sure what kinds of questions they're going to get. "They could ask anything," clients often tell me. Right. That's okay if you're PREPARED for the questions. You're not ready for your presentation if you haven't exhaustively prepared for the questions. Preparing well for Q&A is one of the easiest ways to ensure that your presentation succeeds. We will talk about that later in this chapter.

Learn to Sense When Questions Are Coming

After a recent presentation, one of the attendees came up to me and said, "I'm stumped by something that happened during your presentation. I was about to ask a question. And before I raised my hand, you looked at me and said, 'Do you have a question?' How did you know that?"

He made it seem like I had somehow read his mind, and of course, I hadn't done that at all. I had to think hard to remember the instance he was talking about, but in thinking back on the moment, I did remember noticing that he wrinkled his brow and tilted his head a little, sort of like the puzzled look a dog will sometimes give you.

When I saw that puzzled look, I immediately stopped and said, "Do you have a question?"

I noticed his puzzled look because I've become very attuned to anything that might suggest a question or misunderstanding from the audience. I love getting questions because I know that they're one of the keys to really engaging the audience. So over time, I've learned how to sense the questions just from the looks of my listeners.

This is not a hard skill to learn. Just watch for possible questions in the same way that you might scan the beach for pretty sea shells. To find those shells, you need to be watching for them carefully, because if you miss one, it will be swept away by the next ocean wave. Similarly, you need to be watching your audience for questions. Scan faces for puzzled looks. Watch for hands that are about to go up. As soon you sense a question coming, drop everything and answer it. If you fail to grab it, you'll miss an opportunity.

TO ANSWER QUESTIONS WELL, PREPARE FOR THEM

I was working with the senior VP of sales for a large software company who told me about how he prepared for a sales call on the CEO of a Fortune 50 company. "We had spent two days going through every possible question that he might ask," he told me. "We must have written down 200 questions. We were prepared out the *wazoo!*"

So when the time came for the meeting, the CEO ushered the sales VP into a conference room. There was no small talk at all. The CEO looked at the sales VP and said, "Can you get a job at your company for my son?"

"Now that was one question we hadn't prepared for!" laughed the sales VP.

Everything worked out well in this story as the sales VP helped the CEO's son get a job. But the reason I'm telling you this story is to highlight how the best sellers prepare for a sales pitch. They work very hard at preparing for all possible questions.

You're not prepared for your presentation if you haven't prepared for the questions. Without a doubt, the most important part of any pitch is the questions, so be ready for them.

Guessing the questions you will get is not hard. When I was in law school, I would regularly get together with my friends before exams for intensive study sessions. And during these study sessions, we would spend most of our time doing one thing: guessing the questions. We called this "psyching out the test."

We found that we actually were quite good at psyching out the test. We even guessed that our Constitutional Law professor was going to ask us a question about the famous dissent in the *Roe v. Wade* case. My point is this: if you spend even a little bit of time trying, you can almost always guess what questions you're going to get from your clients.

You don't need to be a mind reader to know what questions they're going to ask. If you have any degree of experience with your subject, you will know the hot buttons.

1. How much does it cost?
2. How long will it take?
3. What are the biggest risks?
4. What are the biggest challenges?

Write out at least twenty questions and practice exactly how you will answer them. When I was practicing law, we commonly would go before appellate courts where we knew that we were going to get barraged by questions from the panel of judges. Our preparation for the oral argument consisted almost exclusively of planning how we would answer key questions.

When I work with teams in helping them prepare for a pitch, I always insist on having the entire team available for a Q&A session. We list possible questions. We discuss who will answer the questions and what they will say.

HOW TO GIVE A GOOD ANSWER: DON'T TELL THEM HOW TO BUILD A WATCH

Giving a correct answer is important. Almost equally important, however, is answering the question in a way that builds confidence. The rule of thumb is this: the tighter the answer, the more confidence you will inspire.

Here's an example of how *not* to inspire confidence with an answer. I was defending one of my firm's largest clients in a lawsuit. I was only a second year lawyer, so it wasn't a particularly important lawsuit in the great scheme of things. But it was an important case to me and I was doing my best and working hard.

One afternoon while in my office, my telephone rang; it was one of the senior partners in the firm who wanted me to come to his office to discuss the case.

Reporting to his office immediately, the senior partner looked at me and said, "Joey, what is happening with the case that you're working on?"

I launched into a five minute dissertation on everything I knew about the case. I told him about the brief I was working on. I told him about all the facts of the case. I told him about the trip I had made down to south Georgia to investigate a couple of the key incidents in the case.

"Joey," the senior partner interrupted. "I've asked you the time of day and you're telling me how to build a watch."

Everything I said was completely accurate. But my rambling answer did not inspire confidence. To the contrary, my rambling made the senior partner wonder whether he had made a mistake in entrusting me with this case. That rambling made me seem uncertain and unconfident.

What would have been a good answer? What would have been an answer that would have inspired confidence? Probably the best answer would have been "We're trying the case next week and we have a 50/50 chance of winning. It all depends on whether our lead witness comes across as believable or not."

When you give a tight answer, there is a sense that you are in control. The listener thinks, "That's a tight answer. He seems to have it all together."

THE MODEL ANSWER: A SENTENCE OR TWO PLUS A BRIEF EXPLANATION

The key to inspiring confidence is to answer the question quickly and then give a brief explanation. Get the basic answer out in the first two sentences. Then give some explanation.

Sample Question I:
"How long will the project take?"

Bad answer: Well, we need to have a couple of meetings with your employees first. During those meetings, we're going to gather a lot of data about their preferences. Sometimes their preferences can dictate a lot of extra work on our part. However, if their preferences are pretty straightforward, we probably won't have to do much in terms of follow up. If that's the case, then we estimate that the project will take between three and six months.

Good answer: "We estimate it will take no more than six months. The key will be whether we can get the key data from your employees in the first two sessions."

Sample Question II:
"How much will the project cost?"

Bad answer: Well, right now we don't have costs for steel. The most important cost on this job will be the steel. That's what we're going to use to erect the core of the building and that is what drives much of our costs. So assuming that we can get those costs within the first week, we'll know. My initial estimate will be $20 million."

Good answer: "Our estimate is $20 million. The key issue there is whether we can get the steel at the cost we expect. We'll know that within the first week of the project."

In each case, the second answer is tight and inspires confidence. The basic answer is out immediately with no beating around the bush. Such tight answers say to the prospect, "I've got this under control."

The bad answers, however, are rambling messes. Sure they're accurate, but the information pours out in dribs and drabs. The speaker unintentionally taunts the listener, slowly parceling out information until finally the answer that everyone longs for arrives.

CAN YOUR ANSWERS PASS THE "CELL PHONE" TEST?

The best answers always pass the "cell phone test."

Imagine that you're on your cell phone, and someone calls you and asks you an important question. Now imagine that you're standing or driving through an area with spotty cell coverage. Knowing that your cell phone could go out at any moment, you're going be sure that you give the basic answer quickly. You don't want your answer cut off in the middle of the sentence.

Getting to the key part of the answer quickly is called "passing the cell phone test." And the best answers always pass.

To Get Good at Answering Questions, Practice the "Two Sentence" Drill

When we coach executives from publicly held companies to speak with Wall Street analysts, one of the key focus areas is answering Q&A. An easy way to get into trouble when speaking to analysts is to start rambling in response to an analyst's question. If you say the wrong thing "off the cuff," it could cause the stock price to stumble. So you need to be disciplined when taking questions.

The best answers are tight and to the point with little elaboration. We prepare using the "two sentence drill."

In this drill, we'll write down thirty possible questions we might expect from the analysts. In responding to each question, the person on the hot seat must give a complete answer in no more than two simple sentences.

You can do the same thing with the Q&A you expect to get during your pitch. For example, here are a few typical questions you might get during a pitch. What would your one-sentence or two-sentence answers sound like?

1. *How much will this cost?* Answer: "We expect the cost to be $10,000 a month. The only variable will be the number of times you call us.

2. *What is the biggest issue you see with finishing the project on time?* Answer. "Our biggest challenge will be the weather. However, if we can get started in the next two weeks, we will be able to get the structure dried in before the weather changes."

3. *What are the biggest risks with closing this deal?* Answer: "The biggest risk is that the financial analysis won't yield

what we expect. We'll be finished with our analysis within two weeks."

Giving a two-sentence answer takes discipline. It's fun and very valuable. It is also one of the little bits of "presentation execution" that separate you from your competition.

I'm not saying that ALL of your answers should be one or two sentences long. I'm merely saying that giving tight answers right at the top of your response builds a sense of confidence. Once you've given your short answer, then you can briefly explain.

Don't feel that you have to go on forever with your explanation. The wonderful thing about Q&A is that there is a built-in safety mechanism to ensure that your listeners are happy with your response. If they're not happy, they can ask a further question!

Assume that the audience wants a short answer. If they want more, they can ask.

WAYS TO FOSTER INTERACTION: TRICKS TO DRAWING OUT THE AUDIENCE

The best way to make the pitch interactive is to leave plenty of time for questions and then handle those questions effectively. But there are other ways to make your presentation interactive. The first thing that we recommend is asking questions of the prospect.

When you stand up to give a presentation, presumably there is a lot of information you don't have that you wish you did have. This is true even if you've done the right things by interviewing the key decision-makers in preparation for your presentation. Indeed, as soon as you're hired, chances are that you are going to sit down with your prospect and have a long meeting, asking for further information and guidance to help you best serve your customer.

One of the best ways to engage the prospect during a pitch is to ask what you would ask in the first meeting once you're hired.

For example, if you're an architect, you're probably going to want to get a sense of the prospect's design priorities. If you're an attorney, you're going to want to get a sense of how much appetite your prospect has for an aggressive litigation strategy. If you're a financial manager, you're going to want to get a stronger sense of your appetite for risk in his or her investments.

We worked recently with an architect who was seeking an opportunity to design a 100,000-square-foot office space for a computer software company. This architect had interviewed the facilities manager, and knew they had a very limited budget. They wanted to make sure that their space looked very well designed, even though they didn't have much money. They wanted "a lot of bang for the buck." "They had $5 million to spend on 100,000 square feet," the architect said. "That's not really a lot of money. I knew they were going to have to make some decisions on where to spend the money. In fact, that was probably the most important decision they were going to have to make."

With that in mind, I suggested that he put that issue to the prospect in the presentation. "Why not ask them where they want the money to be spent?" I said.

That's exactly what this architect did. Indeed, he asked the prospect exactly what he would have asked during the first meeting after being hired. "You've got a limited budget here and you're going to have to make some decisions regarding how to allocate your money," he said. "Let's categorize your space into lobby space, work space, executive offices, conferencing space, and research and development space. Now to help you allocate resources, I'd like you to assign *automobile brands* to coincide with the investment you'd like to go with each space. For example, if you want a very high end lobby, you can assign a Porsche to the lobby. But here's the catch. You can only assign one Porsche. You must also assign one economy car to one of the spaces. Finally, the rest of the assignments must be moderately priced cars. This will give me a sense of how you want to allocate resources."

Making the prospect discuss how they would allocate resources did something very important: it allowed the buyer to glimpse exactly what he was buying. When someone hires an architect they're hiring the intangible ability to create good designs. With that in mind, it's a great idea to "play architect" during the presentation. This gives the prospect a sense of how the project will go.

And that's exactly what this architect did. After getting a sense of where the prospect would allocate resources, he learned that the "Porsche" should be the workspace for the majority of the employees. They didn't care about having a fancy lobby, fancy executive offices, or even fancy research and development space. With that in mind, he went to the flip chart and made a few rudimentary sketches of ideas that would satisfy that need for high-end workspace for the majority of employees. He also showed photographs of high-end workspace designs.

But you don't have to have some clever approach to drawing out your prospect. You can just ask simple, obvious, but important, questions.

I worked with a lawyer who was pitching for the chance to help a large utility comply with a series of new complex federal regulations. During the "bake off" presentation, they made the presentation interactive by simply asking, "So can you tell us what you've done so far in terms of compliance with the regulations?"

It's a great question. If they're eventually hired, they are certainly going to have to know the answer. So why not ask it during the pitch? It's a great way to engage the prospect on a relevant topic. And engaging the prospect is critical.

Foster Interaction by Sending Ahead Something to Discuss

One of the best ways to make sure that your presentation is interactive is to send the prospect something ahead of time with a note saying, "We can discuss this during our meeting."

A consultant I work with is involved in helping pharmaceutical firms comply with FDA rules. When they're hired, they engage in highly complex compliance programs. He says, "When we go in for a sales presentation, we always send ahead a plan for how we will spend the first year of our engagement. Even if they don't read it, it gives us something to discuss with them. It helps make the pitch more like a work session than a pitch."

Virtually any business can use this tactic. If you're an attorney, send ahead a brief outline of thoughts on how to approach winning the lawsuit. If you're an architect, send ahead design ideas that your listeners can react to. If you're a software engineer, send ahead key issues with the software installation that you'd like to discuss.

And don't worry too much about sending out something that the prospect won't initially embrace as the final answer. The point here is not to send out a perfect solution. The point is to give something that will get the conversation started, transforming your presentation from a pitch to a working session.

Ask the Prospect to React to Your Proposed Ideas

Another way to make your presentation interactive is to ask the prospect to react to the ideas that you propose.

If you're proposing a method for streamlining your client's food distribution system, you might outline where you would recommend locating the prospect's distribution centers. Maybe you would even include a map detailing exactly where the distribution centers could be located. Then you would go into the reasons why you think that this particular arrangement would work best for your prospect.

Before moving on, ask the prospect to react to your ideas, but do it in a way that doesn't put them in a position of having to approve or disapprove. The goal here isn't to get them to approve your plan as you lay out the presentation. Of course, they will want things to be different if they actually hire you. The goal is to get a conversation started about the proposal so that they can get a feel for you and your professional intellect.

Here's one way to get the prospect to react without putting her on the defensive. "Now that we've laid out some ideas as a way of getting the conversation started about your project, we'd love to hear your initial reaction."

Just as when you do a trial close at the end of your presentation, interacting with the prospect like this during a presentation will almost always lead to good things. Chances are they're going to like parts of what you propose and dislike other parts. But the most important part is the reaction you give. You need to listen and respond, either adjusting your ideas to meet theirs or justifying your own decisions. Either way, you've got a healthy conversation going, and that's a good thing.

How to Structure an Interactive "First Presentation" to a Prospect

Here's a situation that happens with many of our clients. You're invited to come to a prospect's office to deliver a presentation. The prospect doesn't necessarily think it needs your service. And they're really not interested in giving you much time for discovery before the pitch. They just want you to come in and give a presentation. "Give us your dog and pony show," they say.

In this circumstance, most people come in and give their usual "capabilities presentation." As you know, the problem with "capabilities presentations" is that they often fall flat. They usually don't address the prospect's true needs or focus on the prospect's key challenges. So what do you do?

If this were a competitive pitch, I would recommend that you consider not going at all. If you don't know anything at all about the prospect, then it makes little sense to pitch to them. You have almost no chance of winning the pitch. If you do decide to go, use your business experience and make an educated guess about the prospect's business issues. If you know both your business and your prospect's business well, then guessing isn't such a bad choice.

But there is another choice. You can conduct an interactive discovery session disguised as a sales pitch. In this approach, you deliver a generic solution-oriented capabilities presentation. But in addition to delivering the presentation, make it as interactive as possible.

Use the opportunity to ask the prospect to provide you with the same information you would want during a true discovery session.

So how would this work? You give your three solution-oriented points. But you throw in lots of discovery-oriented questions in addition to success stories.

Do you remember the large information services company that provides background check services for its clients? If you recall, I recommended that their capabilities presentation focus less on products and more on solutions.

In the case of an information services company, they would focus on three key things:

- How we save our clients money
- How we reduce their risk
- How we can improve their systems

In detailing the first section of the presentation, you could explain exactly how you save clients money and give stories that illustrate how you've succeeded with other clients.

Then you could begin to ask the prospect questions designed to determine their needs.

In this case, you might ask, "Approximately how much are you spending per month on background checks?" "What are your biggest costs in this area?" "What are the biggest risks you face in hiring?" "Can you talk to me about your new employee intake process?"

The point is that you get to ask the questions that you would really want to know about their business. The idea is to get a discussion started.

The risk you take with this approach is that you probably won't be able to give them any specific solutions at the pitch. But so what? If this is the first time you're meeting with the prospect, you're not going to get any business from them that day anyway. Why not begin gathering information so that you can possibly help them at some time in the future?

By making the presentation highly interactive, they're going to get a chance to get to know you and presumably they'll begin to like you. When the time comes that they're ready to make a decision, you're going to have the inside track for getting the business.

FINAL THOUGHT ON INTERACTIVITY: IT WINS

One of the fundamentals that distinguishes you from your competition is your ability to make your pitch interactive. The best pitches have the feel of a choreographed chat. Your presentation follows a road map, carefully laying out your points and solutions.

But you're not just barreling down the road without stopping. You're constantly stopping along the way to discuss and raise issues. You're pausing to answer questions. You're chatting your way down the road, constantly making sure your prospect is happy, always clear on where the road leads and why.

If you do your job right, you'll get plenty of interaction from your prospect. Your prospects will get all of their questions answered and you'll increase your chances of winning the business.

Fundamental #5:

Rehearse...
Rehearse...
and Rehearse
Again

CHAPTER 16

Practice Like Crazy

One of the most important things you can do to separate yourself from your competition may also be simplest—rehearse your presentations like crazy. Rehearse every aspect of the pitch. Rehearse the words you're going to say. Rehearse how you and your team will work together. Rehearse how you're going to use your slides. Rehearse exactly where you're going to stand or sit. Rehearse everything.

How does rehearsal separate you? Most presenters don't rehearse much. And a well-rehearsed presentation is very apparent. It's easy to see who has practiced and who is "winging it."

One of the dirty little secrets of my business—the public speaking skills coaching business—is that rehearsal by itself will make most people much better. More important, it will make you come across better to your audience, and if you want to win business that's essential.

Here's an example of how rehearsal can pay off. Standing in a conference room in Nashville, Tennessee, Ed looked terrified. And anxiety is not a pretty thing to see on the face of a construction superintendent. Construction superintendents are some of the most confident people I've ever met. The good ones—and Ed is a great one—have a swagger that's been earned from years of strutting around construction sites, supervising sub-contractors as they build office buildings and hospitals.

So to see Ed with a look of fear in his eyes was a little upsetting. Even though he was a terrific communicator, he clearly was out of his element. Put a hard hat on him and plant him amid stacks of dry wall, and he comes across as a confident leader. Make him wear a dress shirt and slacks while standing in a conference room and suddenly his legs turn to jelly.

What's worse is that a $50 million piece of business all depended on him. Literally. His company was bidding for a chance to build a new hospital in a small town in North Carolina. Anyone in the construction business these days knows that project superintendents play a critical role in the pitches for new construction opportunities. In a sense, they're the star of the show because they're going to be the main person who the building owner will be dealing with on a day-to-day basis. If the owner doesn't like your superintendent, you're not going to win.

So Ed was terrified. He is a terrific superintendent, but it had been a couple of years since he last gave a presentation and that was in his church. In two days, he had to help win a huge opportunity for his firm.

He came through with flying colors. He did so well that when the key decision-maker called the next day, he said, "You got the job on one condition. You have to promise us that Ed is going to be the superintendent. We want him."

What happened? How did Ed go from being a nervous bucket of goo to a confident presenter in two days?

Simple. He executed one of the fundamentals that separate winners from losers in these presentations. He rehearsed like crazy. He had about a ten-minute piece of the presentation and he probably rehearsed it ten times over two days. He rehearsed and rehearsed and rehearsed. "Let's do it again," he said to me after going through it twice. I was ready to take a break and go to lunch. But Ed wanted to do it again. That "We're going to rehearse this until we get it right" attitude is what made the difference.

Was he nervous during the presentation? "I was quite nervous at first," he told me. "But once I got started and the practice kicked in, I settled down. After a while I actually enjoyed it."

I was speaking recently to an account representative for a large marketing agency. He asked me, "What do you do if you just don't have time to rehearse for a pitch?"

I looked at him and with total seriousness told him that, "I really don't have much sympathy for people who won't rehearse for a pitch. What if the New York Giants said, 'What do we do if we don't have time to prepare for next week's game?' I just don't get it. One of your competitors wants the win enough to practice really hard. They're probably going to win."

I hear the same thing over and over from decision-makers who watch competitive pitches. "One team came in and blew everyone else away. They were just so much smoother and better prepared than everyone else." Rehearsal is something that is extremely apparent to people who watch presentations. And it's a huge distinguishing factor.

WHY REHEARSAL SEPARATES YOU
Rehearsal separates you like a Red Delicious apple separates itself on the grocery store shelf.

I love apples. To me, there's nothing better than a sweet, crunchy apple. My mouth is watering as I'm typing these words. I've actually evolved in my taste for apples. I've tried them all.

Braeburn. Gala. Granny Smith. Fuji. You name it.

But I've got an ongoing problem with apples. I have a dickens of a time selecting apples. The problem is that you can't bite into the apple before you buy it. So what do most people (including me for about two years) generally select? Red Delicious. Those gorgeous red shiny apples are the most popular apples in America. They're beautiful.

They're also not particularly tasty when compared to some of the other apples (Fujis are my current favorites). They win the competition for America's business because they look so good. You can't really judge how they taste until you take them home, but you certainly can judge how they look, and they look marvelous.

Your potential customers have the same problem in selecting a product or service. It's very hard to tell which product is going to "taste" the best when brought home. So they are heavily influenced by what they can see. They look for the shiniest apple.

One thing that makes your "apple" shiny is lots of rehearsal. Indeed, when we speak to decision-makers, they regularly tell us that they can always tell which presentations look practiced and which presentations look "on the fly."

I interviewed an assistant general counsel for employment matters at a large retailer. She described conducting a "bake off" for a large litigation matter. Of the two firms on the short list, one was an incumbent firm that had done a lot of work for the retailer in the past and the other was a small, employment litigation boutique firm. The litigation boutique came in extremely well-prepared and obviously well-rehearsed. They had three lawyers in the presentation and they spoke in what was obviously a well-choreographed and rehearsed presentation.

The incumbent then came in and just chatted in an unfocused way about the litigation opportunity. It was obvious that they hadn't done much preparation. All they did was remind them of the work they had done for them in the past.

"When they were done," the assistant general counsel told me, "we all looked at each other and said, 'Well, that was terrible.'" Indeed, the level of preparation by both teams was extremely obvious. The better-prepared, well-rehearsed, non-incumbent firm won the opportunity.

Rehearsal is easy to see and easily measured. That's not to say that preparation alone will win you the business. But it's one of the many little things that, when executed well, will help you stand out from your competition.

How to Rehearse: Practice It Like It's a Play

A good rehearsal is performed aloud, from beginning to end without stopping, just as if it's a play. I'm amazed at how often people don't understand this simple idea.

A team of logistics engineers hired me to help them prepare for a big presentation. They were going to be presenting a new business idea to a corporate board, hoping that they would approve and fund a joint venture with another company. We had worked together in creating the pitch. The actual presentation would be in two days.

I walked into the room and everyone was laughing. They had gotten together two hours earlier to begin their preparations. When I showed up, the team leader looked at me and said, "I think we're just about ready to go. We've actually been rehearsing for the last two hours."

If that were true, I would have been delighted. But before I was going to go home, I wanted to probe a little further. I didn't want them walking into the boardroom in two days unprepared.

"You say you 'rehearsed.' What exactly did you do?" I said.

"We assigned everyone roles in the presentation and we discussed what everyone will say," he told me.

"And what else did you do?"

"What do you mean?" he said.

"Have you actually stood up and gone through the entire presentation as it would appear before the board of directors in two days?" I said.

"Well, no but …"

Hmm.

Let's be clear about this. Rehearsal is not a complex idea. It's practicing the presentation aloud from beginning to end without stopping—as if you were doing it live. Nothing else counts as rehearsal. If you haven't done this, then you're not fully rehearsed. No excuses. End of discussion.

"Discussing what everyone is going to say" is not rehearsal. Nor is flipping through your slides on the airplane. Nor is sending out an e-mail to team members on topics they should expect to cover during the presentation.

I hear many people describe their rehearsal as "figuring out what I'm going to say." By that, they usually mean that they will flip through their slides saying, "I know what I'm going to say here. I know what I'm going to say there," etc. That is not a rehearsal. Sure, you know in general what you're going to talk about when the slide comes up, but you don't know exactly *how you're going to say it.*

Remember! These words have to come out of your mouth. And you want them to come out smoothly and without hesitation. So there is no substitute for practicing the actual words that you're going to say over and over again.

Let's say that you're going to talk about how your plan for building a hospital resembles another project you did last year. How are you going to articulate that thought?

The first time you try to say it, you might start out like this:

Last year we built a hospital with fifteen floors and a cardiac wing in Denver, Colorado. They were very worried about patient safety because the last time they had work done, one of their patients tripped over a stray piece of drywall.

Does that say it the way you want? Maybe.
However, it might sound better if you said it like this:

We understand that you're concerned about safety. We heard about how on a previous project one of your nurses slipped on some paint and sprained her wrist. We actually had another client just like you in Denver. On a previous job, a patient had tripped over some drywall.

I'm not suggesting that one way is right and one is wrong. All I'm saying is that you need to figure out the best way to say the thing—to get the words to come out of your mouth. And you can't do that without rehearsal.

By practicing, you can find all the dead ends where you don't want to go. You can hear how it sounds and say, "That doesn't sound right. I better try that again."

Lots of Rehearsal Doesn't Mean Memorize the Whole Thing

I worked with a senior executive at a telecommunications company who wanted me to help him become a better presenter. He sent me the videotape of a presentation he had given recently. He walked to the front of the stage, looking rather stiff in a pinstripe suit.

Then he proceeded to deliver his presentation in a rather stiff monotone. It was clear he had memorized the entire thing and was reciting it verbatim.

The problem with memorizing your entire prevention is that you sound canned, which can be just as bad as being unprepared. Remember, you want to connect with the prospect and make them believe that you can add value to their business. If you've simply memorized your part, you come across as non-credible. Given enough time, anyone can memorize a presentation on any topic.

You want to come across as someone who can speak intelligently about your topic without excessive prompts.

How do you Rehearse without Memorizing?

People memorize a speech when they write out their script word for word and then commit it to memory. Don't do that. Put together an outline and then simply begin to practice the presentation, figuring out the exact words as you go.

Your outline might look something like this

1   Safety is important to you
2.   How we'll promote safety on the job
3.   How our program will save you money

Once you have the outline in place, you should think of each of the key points as lead-ins for a short section. You might begin practicing like this:

When we met with you last week, you told us that safety was going to be an important issue for you on this job. Indeed, you told us that on your last job, you had a couple of minor injuries. We certainly want to make sure that we do everything possible to ensure that everyone working on and around the job is as safe as possible.

That's why safety is JOB ONE on our worksites. Let me talk about what we're going to do to keep your job safe. Blah. Blah blah.

Next, I'd like to tell you about how our safety program actually will save you money. Blah blah blah.

Then you should practice delivering the presentation several times, working on honing exactly how you say everything. Every time you do it, you'll probably say it a little differently. That's okay. After several tries, you'll settle into a way of speaking that sounds natural and works for you. It won't sound memorized and you'll be ready to deliver it in a way that feels good.

FOR GOODNESS SAKE, DON'T READ YOUR PITCH

Many people like to read their presentations. This is one of the worst things you can do. It's a sure sign that you haven't rehearsed much, and you come across as a total amateur. It eliminates your ability to connect with your audience, because if you're reading, you're not making eye contact.

Make notes and practice your presentation aloud enough times that you can deliver the presentation extemporaneously. If you think you're going to forget something, you can look at your notes.

But, please don't read your presentation. It's one of the true crimes against audiences. I don't need you to read me a presentation. I can read it myself.

REHEARSING AS A TEAM

When it's a team presentation, rehearsal is even more important.

Here's why. Say you're a theater patron on your way to a production of *The Wizard of Oz*. After much hassle, you gather your wife and all three kids in your car and make your way downtown. After finally finding a parking lot, you make your way to a restaurant where you all rush through your meal, worried that you're not going to get there in time to get your seats before the curtain goes up. However, you do get to the theater on time, stopping to buy some candy for the kids before taking your seats.

Finally, you're all in your seats when the theater gets dark and the crowd gets quiet. The curtain goes up and you're beginning to enjoy the show. However, just as Dorothy is about to sing "Somewhere Over the Rainbow," Toto starts barking and running wildly around the stage. It's annoying and ruins the best song in the show.

You think, "Why didn't they get a dog that doesn't bark? And didn't they think of putting a leash on the dog?" In fact, you read in the paper the next day, it was a new Toto for that performance and the old Toto didn't need a leash. Too bad. For your purposes, the whole evening was tainted by that mistake.

I think that presenting teams should exhaustively rehearse their presentations much like a theater company must exhaustively rehearse *The Wizard of Oz*. Unless you rehearse, you never know if "Toto" is going to start barking and running around the stage.

I also think that it's important to rehearse out of respect for the prospect's time. When you go to the theater, you invest a lot, buying dinner for your kids, buying tickets, and giving up an entire evening. You want it to be good. Your prospects also are heavily invested in your presentation. Their time is valuable. They've likely spent a lot of time sifting through RFPs. Often, someone at the prospect company has gone out on a limb to get your firm the chance to pitch. If you go in unprepared, it's highly annoying and you may not get another chance to pitch.

Like the family on the way to the stage show, your prospects want you to succeed. "We want to find someone who will help us," one general counsel told me. "We don't want to spend a lot of our time and not get the right fit. We hope that the presentations blow us away. Unfortunately, it doesn't happen very often."

To raise the chance that you'll blow away your prospect, you need to rehearse as a team. Like stage productions, team presentations have many "moving parts." There are dozens of "Toto" problems that can arise if they're not rehearsed. How should everyone be introduced? How are handoffs to be handled? What do we do about the fact that we only have thirty minutes to present and seven people on the presenting team? Who is going to handle the "how much does it cost" question? How do we ensure that no one disagrees with each other in front of the prospect?

Remember that your prospect is most likely not well-acquainted with your team. They don't know how well you work together. And they can't really know without hiring you, but they can judge how well your team performs during the pitch. If you're interrupting and contradicting each other, what does that say about your firm? The natural judgment is, "If they can't deliver a well-constructed pitch, how are they going to build my building?" On the other hand, if you deliver the presentation like a well-oiled machine, what does it say about your team? Obviously, it makes the prospect think, "This team knows how to work together. There's a good chance they'll work together well during our project."

KEYS TO PRESENTING WELL AS A TEAM: KNOW YOUR ROLES AND STICK WITH THEM

The key to presenting well as a team is for everyone to know their roles and stick to those roles.

I worked with an architecture firm in which several of the architects told me about how they had a senior partner who would ruin almost every presentation they delivered as a team. The typical presentation would include a lead architect, a project manager, a lead technical architect, and this senior partner. The project manager told me about what would regularly happen during the presentations. The senior partner would open the presentation, and introduce all of the supporting players.

"Like clockwork," the project manager said, "at some point during the presentation, [the senior partner] will interrupt and take over, correcting us and generally acting like he is the star of the show. We always felt like idiots. We almost never won. It was ridiculous."

This is the exact reason you need to rehearse as a team. Everyone needs to know their roles and stick to their roles.

PRESENTATION TEAM ROLES

Who should be the Anchor? The anchor should be the highest ranking person who is going to be actively involved in the project. If the firm's managing partner is not going to be involved in doing the work, she shouldn't be the anchor. Prospects tell us over and over that they have no interest in hearing from senior partners who are there just for show.

Starting the Presentation: As noted in section 1, the presentation should begin by focusing on the business problem at hand. However, many people want to know exactly what to say at the beginning of the presentation. We recommend a simple, "Hello. We're from Smith and Richardson. And thank you for allowing us to compete for this opportunity." From there you will go into the true "hook" of your presentation. It might be something like this: "When we spoke last week, you told us that the biggest concern that you have with this project is making a decision that will make you more competitive as a firm."

Introducing the Team Members: After previewing your message with the three core points, it's important to introduce the team. I recommend beginning by saying something like this: *"Before we get into the body of the presentation, let me introduce the people who will be working with you. We think they bring a lot of talent to help you achieve your goals."* Then, as you introduce them, be sure that you do more than just give the experience of each team member. Be sure you highlight the *relevant experience* they will bring to solving the unique problems faced by the prospect. For example, you might say, *"Jim Rogers is going to be the superintendent on this job. Jim has a lot of experience working on the kind of hospital expansion you're facing. In fact, Jim is very experienced bringing in projects ahead of schedule, just as we hope to do with you. On his last job, he brought in Mount Wilson Hospital two months ahead of schedule. He's going to do a great job for you."*

Transitions: The key to a good transition is taking the opportunity to re-focus on the core message of the presentation. Don't just say, "Now, let's turn it over to Janet who will be your project manager." That does move along the presentation; however, it doesn't reinforce any key themes. Try something like this: *"Now we're going to turn it over to Janet who will be your project manager. As project manager, it will be Janet's job to ensure that you don't have any surprises during the course of the project."*

Distributing Questions: Sometimes it's obvious who should handle a particular question. "What do you see as the biggest challenge in coming up with the correct budget?" In the construction business, that's an estimator question. However, sometimes you're going to get questions where it's not completely clear who should step up. "How do we make sure that we hit our schedule?" That could go to the superintendent or the project manager. It's the anchor's job to say, *"Why don't we let Jack, our project manager handle that one."* And the anchor's decision is final! No second-guessing during the presentation. It makes you look like a bunch of amateurs.

Role-players: The most important thing that the role-players must do is hit their messages and stay within their time limits. One of the classic ways that presentations go awry is when team members go too long. It's important to show discipline and stick with the time limits.

Rehearsing Questions as a Team: Don't Skimp Here

One of the most important things you can do as a team is to rehearse how to handle questions. First, you should seek to anticipate all possible questions. Then you need to come up with who will take the questions and how the questions will be answered.

Start by brainstorming all possible questions. As a team, you should be able to come up with a good list of all possible questions. There is almost no excuse for being surprised by questions. If you're good at what you do, you should be able to anticipate virtually all questions that your prospect should ask. Make a long list. As soon as you think you have them all, add ten more.

Next, you should talk through the best answers to the questions. During my law practice days, we would prepare for our oral argument presentations by gathering in a conference room and writing down all the possible questions. Then we would spend hours debating exactly how we would answer each question. We knew that how well we answered those questions would determine whether we won the case. The same holds true with team presentations. You need to plan exactly what you will say to each possible question. How well you plan your answers can determine whether you'll win the job.

Finally, spend time deciding who will take which questions. Pitches often go awry when different members of the pitch team each take a shot at answering a question. Having more than one person tackle a question makes your team look disorganized.

Sometimes team members make the mistake of correcting each other. "Actually, let me see if I can correct Jim on this issue…" This type of intra-team conflict erupts in front of clients all the time. It's disastrous. It makes your team look like the Keystone Kops. No one wants to hire a team that can't get along.

COMPLETE DRESS REHEARSALS AS A TEAM

We recommend two or three complete dress rehearsals from beginning to end without stopping. Most businesses don't actually run through the entire pitch, but a complete dress rehearsal is critical.

You need to have a strong feeling for how the entire presentation flows. You need to have a sense of who is going to speak too long. You need to actually hear everyone's individual messages and make sure that they don't conflict in any way. If one of your team members suggests that the project will be close to budget and another suggests that there is money to be saved in one phase of the project, you want to make sure that you reconcile those ideas.

The best way to ensure that your presentation comes off well is by rehearsing. We say, "Rehearse as if your cash flow depended on it."

Selling Power Magazine once interviewed me about what it takes to be successful at presenting sales pitches as a team. The first question the reporter asked was, "What is the most important thing to do to be successful when presenting as a team?"

That was an easy one. "The most important thing that you should do to succeed as a team is to rehearse," I said.

There was silence on the line. I could tell that the reporter didn't really care for the answer.

"Well, I know that rehearsal is important, but wouldn't you say that how you orchestrate everyone as they speak is important too?"

"No," I insisted. "Without a doubt, the most important thing to succeeding as a team is rehearsal."

Apparently, she didn't care for my answer. Maybe she didn't think that she could lead her article simply telling everyone to rehearse. So she tried a different tactic. "Well, let's assume that everyone is in a different city," she said. "And let's assume that because all the team members can't get together, they won't be able to rehearse in preparation for the presentation. Then what should they do?"

"If they can't rehearse, they need to lower their expectations of winning," I told her. "It's that important."

Can You Practice too Much?

The late-comedian George Carlin used to do a hilarious routine called "Phrases that no one has ever said before." The words were things like, "Please saw my legs off," "Hand me that piano," and "Do what you want to the girl but leave me alone."

I'd like to add another phrase that you'll never hear anyone say, "We lost this opportunity because we rehearsed our presentation too much."

Many people do ask me, however, whether they should be careful not to "practice too much." My answer is always the same. "No. You should practice way too much. Practice until you can do it in your sleep. Practice like your cash flow depends on it."

The idea that you can somehow rehearse "too much" is absurd and sounds more like an amateurish excuse from an inexperienced or simply misguided team leader.

Of course, you can practice yourself into exhaustion. That's not a good thing. I've heard of teams finishing their presentations at 2 in the morning, only to have the team leader say, "Everyone needs to run home and get a few hours sleep. We'll get together at 7 am for a rehearsal. That will have us ready for the presentation at 10 am."

That's not rehearsing too much. That's poor planning of your presentation. If you haven't built in enough time for a couple of good rehearsals, chances are that you're not in a good position to win anyway.

Where do We Sit During the Presentation?

I get this question a lot and there is no simple answer because all rooms are different. In general, you want to be sitting or standing together so that you can all get up and get back down quickly and easily as you transition between speakers.

Far more important is what you should be doing when you're not actually speaking. You should be watching your fellow presenters, paying close attention. You want to look like you're part of the team, not just waiting for your chance to speak.

I've seen team members working their BlackBerries while waiting for their turn to speak. It looks terrible and reflects poorly on the team.

Final Thoughts on Practicing Like Crazy

Anyone can improve dramatically if they practice effectively. I've seen it happen over and over again. A terrible speaker practices like crazy and becomes a teriffic speaker. Just as important, your level of rehearsal is something that comes across very clearly whenever you stand in front of a panel of decision-makers.

The well-rehearsed presenters always stand out from the ones who choose to "wing it." So rehearse. Give your presentation to your wife, your husband, your significant other, your kids, or your dog. Get their feedback. Listen to it. Rehearse as if your cash flow depended on it.

CHAPTER 17

Managing Nerves and Anxiety

No one needs to be reminded of the challenge that anxiety poses in presentations. The number one fear of the average person is public speaking. That's ahead of death and spiders. Everyone, including me, gets nervous when giving a speech. Stage fright affects people in different ways. People get dry mouth, knocking knees, flushed faces, etc. I worked with a woman who told me that she literally forgets everything. "I can't remember my own name," she said. "And I completely blank out on what I'm going to say."

You can't completely eliminate public speaking anxiety. However, there are several things you can do to help yourself perform well in spite of your nerves.

Practice is the Most Important Way to Reduce Anxiety

By far the most important thing you can do to alleviate your nerves is to practice. Whenever I hear that someone gets incapacitated by nerves, the first thing I ask is if they rehearse their presentations.

I worked with the woman who told me she got so nervous during presentations that she simply couldn't perform. She was a senior vice president at a large financial services firm. She came to me because she was about to give a keynote presentation at a very important national trade conference. She was going to introduce a new product from her firm, and she was petrified.

"I'm a terrible presenter," she told me. "I get so nervous that I forget everything I'm going to say." By that, she meant that she would get so nervous that she literally couldn't remember anything at all. "I forget my own name," she said.

"Do you rehearse?" I said.

"Absolutely," she said without blinking. "I always rehearse."

Now that really bothered me. That was inconsistent with my world view. I have always felt that if you practice a lot, you're going to do well. That's it. No exceptions. Here is someone who is telling me that she practices a lot and yet still is a bad presenter.

"How exactly do you practice?" I asked.

"Well, I always do it the same way," she said, "I take out my deck of slides and go through them several times in my head. I then close the door of my office and lie down on my sofa. I then think about my presentation with my eyes closed. It's sort of like meditation."

Huh? "That's not a rehearsal," I told her. "That's a nap."

We had her rehearse the presentation out loud a dozen times from beginning to end without stopping. She went to the presentation and did great. She actually did so well that her firm now uses her as a national spokesperson for this new product. She now travels the country delivering speeches.

The point of this story is that rehearsal alone allowed her to overcome her anxiety. To be sure, she still felt nerves.

I've seen it happen dozens of times. Rehearse and you'll be able to perform well in spite of your nerves.

PRACTICE WITH THE TELEVISION ON

I spoke once with a sports psychologist about how great athletes overcome performance anxiety. She told me that the key was simply to rehearse your athletic moves so extensively that you develop a muscle memory that kicks in despite the nerves. She told me about working with Olympic divers as they prepared for competition. "They practice their dives so much that the complex moves in the dives happen automatically, despite enormous pressure," she told me.

And that is the same principle behind rehearsing presentations. You need to practice so often that you develop something akin to what an athlete calls "muscle memory." You need to be able to present despite the intense distraction of anxiety.

We recommend practicing several times and then trying to deliver your presentation with the television playing. Nerves constitute a very disconcerting distraction. A television is also a distraction, and if you can nail your presentation despite a distraction like Larry King going on in the background, chances are that you'll be able to deliver your presentation despite a distraction like stage fright.

PRACTICE THE FIRST MINUTE THE MOST

If you are going to rehearse your entire presentation ten times, then you need to rehearse the first minute of your presentation the most. You're more nervous at the beginning of the presentation than at any other time. And if you nail it, chances are that you'll relax. That will also make your audience relax. If you screw up early, you're going to tighten up. That will also make your audience tighten up. "Oh, my," the audience thinks. "This person is nervous and this is going to be a difficult time."

Whenever I'm nervous, I repeat my opening three lines over and over again in my head. I want to nail that opening because I know that if I get off on the right foot, I usually get on a roll and do well. I remember once, I had to deliver a speech to a Rotary Club at the Holiday Inn in Suwanee, Georgia. I was nervous. Really nervous. I can't exactly remember why I was so nervous. I've spoken so many times that I don't usually get much more than a few butterflies.

And I knew that my first line was going to be, "There was a study done by a researcher at UCLA about the way we communicate. The study found that 55% of the impression we make is based on how we look."

While driving out to the hotel, I must have said that line twenty-five times. I had to wait another forty minutes once I got there because they served lunch before my keynote presentation. During lunch, I probably said that line in my head another fifteen times.

Finally, the moment arrived. I stood up and waited for the applause from my introduction to die down. I then paused and launched into my opening just as I had rehearsed it. It came out smoothly. And I immediately felt myself getting calmer. I knew everything was going to go well. That's the power of really knowing that opening. It sets you up for success.

Physical Keys to Reducing Nerves

The single best way to deal with nerves is to rehearse extensively. However, rehearsal doesn't completely eradicate anxiety. The next key to reducing your nerves is to do a series of physical things.

The physical anxiety you feel when you present is adrenaline. When you get up to speak, a primitive part of your brain identifies what it considers a "dangerous situation" and sends out a "fight or flight" signal calling for adrenaline.

In pre-historic times, that adrenaline would come in handy. Chances are you'd only feel that adrenaline rush if you were being chased by a bear or a tiger. You needed that energy to run away, climb a tree, or win a fight to the death with a cougar. Not any more. Today, that adrenaline just sits in your body and makes your heart race, your mouth dry, and your stomach do somersaults.

So what do you do to counter the adrenaline? Do what your body wants—exercise. Use that adrenaline productively. Climb a flight of stairs. Walk around the block. Comedian Billy Crystal gets quite nervous before going on stage for a live performance. To settle his nerves, he does large numbers of push-ups before every live performance.

Do something to flush out some of that adrenaline. I know an author who gets extremely nervous every time he gets up to give a speech. "When I'm sitting waiting for my turn to speak, I've found that I can do isometric exercises in my seat," he told me. "I tighten my leg muscles and place my hands in my lap and press my palms together, clenching my chest and arm muscles. It helps me deal with my nerves."

COMBINE PRACTICE AND EXERCISE

You can exercise and practice at the same time, giving yourself a double hit of nerve protection. I find that I'm most nervous when I'm speaking at hotels where my client usually has gathered a large group of people. The great thing about hotels is that they have many hallways. If I'm really nervous, I go on long hikes throughout the hotel. However, I don't just walk. I also practice as I go, repeating the key sections.

By show time, I'm ready.

Audience Focus Reduces Nerves

My final bit of advice for dealing with nerves has to do more with an attitude shift than a specific tactic for addressing anxiety. I've found one of the most important ways to deal with nerves is simply to focus less on yourself and more on how you're going to help your audience.

I understand that anxiety is real. I feel it all the time. However, it is a selfish feeling. You're nervous because you're worried about what people will think about you. I find it helpful to remember that presenting and pitching, when done correctly, aren't about you. It is about the audience, and how you will help them.

If you're an attorney, you're pitching for the chance to help a client win a lawsuit. If you're an architect, you're proposing a way to create a more inviting and creative workspace. If you're an accountant, you're proposing ways to help the prospect put in place better financial controls.

If you believe in what you do, then you should believe that you're in a position to help your prospect. The pitch is part of the process of helping. After all, that pitch is when you first show how you're going to be a true partner. If you focus on helping, the anxiety tends to drop off.

"Self talk" also helps deal with nerves. Try saying something like:

"I'm the one in the best position to help these people. I'm just going to do everything I can to help them and speak with as much energy as possible. After that, there's nothing else I can do."

I use words similar to those whenever I'm particularly nervous about a presentation. Sometimes I abbreviate it to, *"I'm just going to do everything I can to help these folks."* Those words help me a lot. And I've found that many of my clients find it helpful as well.

This is not to say that you can say those words alone and eliminate nerves. You still need to rehearse your presentation. No matter how much you rehearse, and no matter how much physical exercise you do, you're still going to have residual anxiety, which will always be with you, probably for the rest of your professional career.

To help you past that final hump, we recommend simply giving yourself a pep talk, and getting yourself to remember that presenting and pitching is about helping your audience members achieve their goals. If you focus on helping them and not on your own anxiety, you'll get through.

Key to Eliminating Anxiety Forever

So far, we discussed tactics to help you perform well despite your nerves. Practice and exercise will reduce anxiety and allow you to perform well. Those tactics won't make you anxiety free. The only way to reduce and eventually *eliminate* anxiety is to speak a lot. I've been speaking several times a week for years and I still get nervous. To be sure, I'm far less nervous than I was in the past. The reduction in anxiety is the result of becoming acclimated to the challenges of speaking. That acclimation happened only because I speak so often. In other words, I'm just getting use to it.

If you want to get to the point where you just don't get nervous at all, there is really only one prescription: speak a lot. Volunteer to speak whenever possible. Join Toastmasters. Get in your firm's speakers bureau. Nothing else is going to make the nerves go away forever.

Conclusion

The great Green Bay Packers had a simple play that was their "bread and butter" on offense. They called it the Power Sweep, the Packer Sweep, or the Lombardi Sweep.

Whatever the name, it was the same basic play. When the ball was snapped to the quarterback, the guards on the offensive line would pull up and all run in the same direction to the left or right, heading toward the sideline as the ball was handed off to the running back. The ball carrier would then follow the guards as they blocked the way.

It was a common play. The defenses would always know it was coming. In fact, the linebackers, when they were playing Packers, would constantly shout, "Watch for the sweep!"

Almost every time, the play would gain five or six yards. Why? Execution. The Lombardi Packers could execute the fundamentals better than the competition. Execution of those fundamentals separated the Green Bay Packers from the other teams.

Similarly, if you want to separate yourself from your competition in a new business pitch, you need to execute the fundamentals described in this book.

Fundamental number one: Make sure your presentation focuses on one thing: your prospect's needs. No one cares about your firm's history. Your prospect only cares about how you will help them solve their business problems.

Fundamental number two: Keep your message simple. Most presentations are too complex and try to make too many points. Your message will stand out if it's simple and disciplined.

Fundamental number three: Show passion. Most presenters speak with a boring "serious" business voice. You will separate yourself if your voice and face show that you really want this job. Be intense. Be passionate.

Fundamental number four: Make the presentation as interactive as possible. Interaction allows the prospect to get a true sense of who you really are. That separates you from the competition.

Fundamental number five: Rehearse. One of the best ways to show that you really care is to come in well practiced. It's always apparent to the prospect who has rehearsed the most. That is another separator.

Execute these fundamentals every time you deliver a pitch and you'll win more than your fair share of presentations.

About the Author

Joey Asher is president of Speechworks, a communication and selling skills coaching firm that helps sales people, professionals, and executives learn how to create and deliver business presentations that win new business.

He has helped clients win billions of dollars in new business contracts and has worked with clients in a wide variety of industries including construction, real estate, architecture, financial services, insurance, high tech, cable, law, accounting, and consulting.

Joey's first book, *Even a Geek Can Speak: Low-Tech Presentation Skills For High-Tech People,* published by Persuasive Speaker Press, is in its third printing. His second book, *Selling and Communication Skills for Lawyers,* was released in 2005 by American Lawyer Media.

Joey's background is both as an attorney and a newspaper reporter. He worked as an adjunct professor of law at Emory University School of Law and was an attorney at Troutman Sanders L.L.P in Atlanta. Prior to law school, he worked as a newspaper reporter for the Gannett newspaper chain in Georgia and New York. Joey graduated from Cornell University and Emory University School of Law.

Joey now lives in Atlanta with his wife Johanna and children Benjamin, Elliott and Annie.

About Speechworks

Speechworks has been helping clients create and deliver winning presentations since 1986. Offerings include small on-camera workshops, seminars for larger groups, and one-on-one executive coaching. They also consult on specific presentations and coach teams as they prepare for new business pitches. To learn more about Speechworks go to *www.speechworks.net* or call 404-266-0888

ASHER COMMUNICATIONS